올드 코리아

원서 복원판

1판 1쇄 2020년 6월 10일
1판 2쇄 2020년 6월 30일

지은이 | 엘리자베스 키스, 엘스펫 키스 로버트슨 스콧

펴낸이 | 류종필
편집 | 이정우, 정큰별
마케팅 | 김연일, 김유리
표지·본문 디자인 | 박미정

펴낸곳 | (주) 도서출판 책과함께
　　　　주소 (04022) 서울시 마포구 동교로 70 소와소빌딩 2층
　　　　전화 (02) 335-1982
　　　　팩스 (02) 335-1316
　　　　전자우편 prpub@hanmail.net
　　　　블로그 blog.naver.com/prpub
　　　　등록 2003년 4월 3일 제25100-2003-392호

ISBN 979-11-88990-74-0 04910
ISBN 979-11-88990-72-6 (세트)

* 이 책은 엘리자베스 키스와 엘스펫 키스 로버트슨 스콧이 1946년 허친슨 출판사Hutchinson & Co., Ltd.에서
　펴낸《올드 코리아 Old Korea》를 원서 그대로 복원한 것입니다.

OLD KOREA

First Published 1946

Also by Elizabeth Keith and Elspet Keith Robertson Scott
EASTERN WINDOWS
AN ARTIST'S NOTES OF TRAVEL IN JAPAN
HOKKAIDO, KOREA, CHINA, AND THE PHILIPPINES

Viscount Kim Yun-Sik

ONE of the most interesting and significant aspects of the Korean Independence Rising was the part taken by some members of the ancient aristocracy. This is a portrait of one of the aged Viscounts, an account of whose action is given in Chapter 6.

Frontispiece

VISCOUNT KIM YUN SIK

OLD KOREA

The Land of Morning Calm

by

ELIZABETH KEITH

and

ELSPET KEITH ROBERTSON SCOTT

with

Notes by *Bishop Cecil* (37 years in Korea), the late *Dr. James Gale* (author of many works on Korea, where he lived for 40 years), *M. Yanagi* (author of a life of William Blake), *Dr. Frank Schofield* (formerly of the Severance Hospital, Seoul), and *Dr. Alice B. Appenzeller*, of Honolulu (who was born in Korea and was for 20 years president of Ewha college for women in that country)

HUTCHINSON & CO. (Publishers) LTD.
LONDON   NEW YORK   MELBOURNE   SYDNEY   CAPE TOWN

DEDICATION

I HAVE a happy recollection of the kind hospitality of ADMIRAL NIMITZ and his wife when I was in Manila. I like to think that when the Atlantic Charter was signed, by the two greatest men of our time, my print, 'The Cock Fight, Manila,' was hanging in the dining saloon of the now historic U.S.S. *Augusta*.

Of GENERAL MACARTHUR, I have the pleasant knowledge that he has some of my prints in his collection.

This book is dedicated to GENERAL DOUGLAS MACARTHUR, LORD LOUIS MOUNT-BATTEN, and ADMIRAL CHESTER NIMITZ, and to all men under their command who were the means of freeing Korea from her oppressor. Korea must be for ever indebted to them.

TEXT CONTENTS

PICTURES IN COLOUR

WATER COLOURS IN MONOCHROME
Between pages 64-65 and 68-69

Artist's Introduction

THESE sketches were made during various visits to Korea and some of them are of my earliest impressions of the country. They had to be chosen for their subject matter, often from a mass of unfinished studies. During the war years my desire was to bring the sympathetic eyes of a world already sated with tales of horror, to this little known land, and I had to use the material at hand. The sketches in monochrome have suffered most, for Korea demands colour. Nevertheless I am grateful in these difficult days to be able to present as many as sixteen colour plates. Through the medium of these pictures I have tried to give glimpses of the dress, homes, customs, and general culture of the Korean people.

By the kindness of various Koreans who posed in old style costumes I was able to get glimpses of the past. Some of these sittings, for example that of the famous scholar, the late Viscount Kim-Yun-Sik, who sat for me in Court Dress, had to be brief. He was then very old and had not long been released from prison.

My sister and I had arrived in Korea at a tragic time—about a month after the Independence Movement demonstrations throughout the country. There were thousands of Korean patriots, even school children, in prison, and many Koreans were being tortured, although not one of them had used any kind of violence. They had done no more than march in procession waving Korean flags and shouting *Mansei*! (Long Live Korea!). We heard many stories of heroism. Not a few people were killed. Yet in the calm faces of the Koreans there was nothing to show what they were thinking and suffering. I sketched one woman of distinction who had been tortured in prison, but bore no hate towards the Japanese.

Everything we heard made us admire the fortitude of the people. Their land had been taken from them by trickery; their Queen had been murdered; they were forbidden to wear their native dress; the school-children were forced to speak Japanese. Many times I have seen men in the white national costume with their coats splashed with ink. Because the Japanese were trying to destroy Korean national individuality, the police had orders to commit these outrages.

The ordinary, unthinking Japanese speaks of the Koreans with contempt, for there had long been a studied propaganda against them. But educated Japanese have respect, even reverence, for Korean art and culture. Korean history goes back much farther than that of Japan.

On my last visit to Seoul I found that all the young Korean men in the 'foreign style' stores could speak English as well as Japanese, but in every trade and profession the Koreans were discriminated against.

Had it not been for the kindness of American and British missionaries I should never have been able to secure subjects for sketching. Indeed, I could not have got near the Korean people so as to obtain a sympathetic understanding of them.

From time to time I have had letters from unknown friends who have bought my prints of Korean subjects. I remember how the late Kermit Roosevelt wrote that he 'revelled in all the homely details of the "Korean Wedding Feast".' My most recent appreciative message is from Owen Lattimore, the well-known authority on China.

The United States was the hope of all persecuted Koreans. It was easy to slip over the border into China, but America was always the goal. The Korean settlement in Honolulu testifies that their hopes were not in vain. Thousands of Koreans there owe their lives and happiness to the United States, and there are many Koreans on the American mainland.

Although Koreans of the last decade may not have appreciated her art treasures as they should have done—the finest paintings, pottery, and sculpture having been taken to Japan—I hope the first act of justice will be the return of these stolen possessions to their birthplace, Korea.

When, on my last visit to Honolulu in 1936, I exhibited my latest as well as my earliest prints at the lovely Museum of Fine Art presented by the late Mrs. Cooke, the Hawaii Koreans invited me to a party at which I showed them the complete set of Korean subjects from which those reproduced in this book are a selection.

Many of the young Koreans had never seen their own country, but nevertheless they were wearing their national dress.

The figure of a cock on the cover is such as is to be seen in the animal and bird emblems in colour on shutters and pictures in domestic interiors.

The black and white decorations of the chapters I have adapted from old Korean screens, woodcuts and crude coloured folk-art house decorations.

Foreword by Bishop Cecil

I HAVE read the manuscript of this book, written by one who was indeed only a visitor to Korea for a few months, but in those months events were happening which made the time a milestone in Korean history.

Outwardly, the 'Independence Movement' of 1919 produced no effect except greater repression, stricter regulations, and, for thousands, untold suffering, loss of personal liberty, or death. Spiritually it stirred up and strengthened throughout Korea the sense of national unity and desire for independence and national expression which no repressive measures could stifle. Korea, with a population of between 24,000,000 and 25,000,000, ranks about twelfth among the nations of the world. Occupied by Japan since 1905, and formally annexed as a province of the Japanese Empire since 1910, it is almost unknown to the Western World, yet it may well be called the strategic centre of the Far East, for its northern borders are conterminous with China and Russia, and its southern coast is only 150 miles from Japan.

The Chino-Japanese and Russo-Japanese wars both began in Korea.

To-day, when Japan has been defeated, Korea waits for the fulfilment of the guarantee given by the Cairo Conference, that her status as an independent nation will be restored in due course.

How this is to be accomplished, what form of government will be established, how far the Korean people are capable of becoming a politically and economically stable nation, from what sources and to what extent advice and assistance will be needed, are all vitally important problems, owing to the strategic position of the country.

Although a quarter of a century has passed since the events related in this book took place, and during these years great changes have occurred in the material development of 'The Land of Morning Calm,' and efforts to suppress national customs, traditions, and language of Korea were intensified, the Koreans still retain their distinctive characteristics which differentiate them from both the Japanese and Chinese.

If it be true that trials and adversities help to show what men's characters really are, then the character of the Koreans depicted in this book help to show us the true spirit of Korea. Mrs. Robertson Scott writes only of what she saw and heard while staying in Korea for a short time, but as I read the manuscript, I, who made Korea my home thirty-seven years ago, felt myself taken back to those tragic days, with its many heroes and heroines.

The post-War future of many nations, far better known than Korea, engages the interest of the world, but the future of few if any of them may be of equal importance with that of Korea ; and it is in hopes of rousing greater knowledge of, interest in, and sympathy for Korea that the author (editor of the Korean classic, *The Cloud Dream of the Nine, Eastern Windows*, etc.) gives this book to the world.

Preface by Mrs. Robertson Scott

IN Far Eastern Asia the peninsular country of Korea, which is slightly less in size than Great Britain, runs south from the mainland between Manchuria and Japan, and is 11,000 miles from Great Britain and 5,000 from the United States.

The Koreans stirred themselves slowly from their sleep of the Middle Ages. Unlike Japan, who awoke to find a glad, kind, if somewhat condescending world, ready with hand outstretched to guide her in the ways of new and strange civilisations, Korea was roused by the stamp of arméd men, and the cry of a murdered Queen. She found herself helpless before a military equipment which transcended her own by years of material progress.

The Koreans have a history of 4,500 years. Racially they belong to the great Chinese family, and it is through Chinese influence that they early adopted Confucianism.

It was in 1895 that Japanese agents murdered the Korean Queen Min, a woman of high intelligence, force of character, and passionate patriotism, who saw the danger to her country and hated the ingratiating Japanese.

Western civilisation may be said to have made its entry into Korea in 1904, when Imperial Russia threatened her southern neighbours. An alert Japan was quick to see that a friendly Korea was a necessity if she was to hold her own against Russia.

Korea, also realising the danger of the Russian menace, willingly allied herself with Japan, lent money to the Japanese Government, allowed the passage of troops and war material through her country, and supplied troops to fight alongside the Japanese. All this, with a friendly China in the background, helped Japan to score a victory over Russia, but the Japanese never repaid the money borrowed from Korea, nor did she acknowledge Korea's share in the victory.

Japan's next move was to send her astute Prince Ito to represent her in Korea on the plea of helping Korea to master the ways of modern government. The Western nations, who then admired the 'gallant little Japs', applauded Japan's action, and the general opinion was that Japan was the best tutor for Korea who had lagged so far behind in the modern race.

The Korean Emperor and his Ministers wished, however, to rule their country in their own way, and one of the most enlightened Ministers, Prince Min Yong Whan, committed suicide in protest against Japan's seizure of power. The Emperor resolutely refused to sign a treaty presented by Ito, but he was too old and weak, without the aid of his able Queen, to override Japanese cunning and pertinacity.

It must be recognised also that Ito was a far-seeing statesman, and that if he had remained longer in Korea things might have gone better for the people, but their intense hatred of the Japanese was deeply rooted.

Korea had herself to blame for her long sleep, and to the indifferent outside world there was nothing of which she seemed so much in need as the pinching and prodding of the clever, militarily disciplined, unresting Japanese.

I may repeat an old story of a conversation between two well-known men, Dr. Gale and Baron Yun-Che-Ho, as they were sailing one day on the Yalu River, just after the Russo-Japanese war. The two friends had been discussing Korea's future. The Baron had been educated and had travelled in the West, and he knew that Korea was not then ready to stand alone against the pressure of the modern world.

Said Dr. Gale to the Baron, 'If you fear that your country will be dominated either by

Russia or by Japan, which of the two Powers would you prefer to dominate her ?' The Baron made no reply for a little time, and then said in a thoughtful tone, 'If Russia dominates us we shall have an easy time but we shall learn nothing. If Japan dominates us, she will comb us as with a fine tooth comb, but we shall make progress.'

Alas, the Baron's prophetic 'fine tooth comb' proved to have teeth of steel ! He himself had reason to remember his own words during the time of the Conspiracy Trial in 1912 when, blameless, he was unjustly sentenced to ten years' penal servitude.

Japanese officials, even those in Korea, were by no means all monsters. There were even Japanese who appreciated Korea too well ! Among these are her students of ancient Korean culture and treasures. The best, the most lovely, specimens of Korean pottery, bronze and carved wooden figures, were removed from the Peninsula and added to Japan's art treasures. The temples at Horiuji in Japan bear witness to the wealth of ancient Korean culture.

The tale has so often been told of how Japanese admirers of Korean art of about 1598 showed their appreciation. Koreans had been the inventors of a lovely, delicate porcelain of a pastel shade. The Japanese coveted this pottery with such intensity that they not only removed the pottery but carried off the potters also and established them at Satsuma in Japan, which has given its name to a porcelain made there. Ancient Korean 'Satsuma' was exquisite ; the modern Japanese variety is greatly inferior.

Unarmed, Korea has had to take the buffetings and contemptuous kicks of her ancient enemy, but within her heart and soul every insult has been registered. Many of her people were dispossessed of their land and their homes. Thousands of Koreans trekked on foot hungry and almost penniless over the bleak mountain border of Manchuria. At times it has seemed as if heaven and earth were deaf to the sorrows of Korea. Slowly a new spirit awoke. From north to south, from east to west, the message ran, and on the first day of March, 1919, came the great day of the Independence Rising.

This book is an account of what was happening in Korea during my three months' stay there in March, April and May of 1919, after staying in Japan for nearly five years, mostly in Tokyo. Like the apostles of old, our hearts 'burned within us' as we heard the stories that poured into the Mission where we boarded, of imprisoned students, of tortured men and heroic girls, both 'heathen' and Christian, subjected to many indignities.

The notes made while in Korea are records of what happened within our immediate knowledge or from information gathered daily by us.

We had introductions to many important Japanese officials and were treated with courtesy by all to whom we made ourselves known. Far from having any prejudice against Japan, we had gone to Korea with the kindliest feeling towards the Japanese for we had many good Japanese friends in Tokyo. We were prepared to believe that Korean troubles were probably exaggerated.

My sister, whose colour prints of Korea and Koreans have since become widely known in the Far East, in America and in Great Britain, stayed in the Far East for some years after my three months' holiday in Korea had ended.

A portion of Chapter 7 is reproduced from an article of mine in the New York magazine, *Asia*.

My sister and I desire to express our indebtedness to Bishop Cecil, Father Lee, Miss Appenzeller, and Miss Elizabeth Roberts for their kind help.

Chapter One ✤ Seoul

AFTER four years' stay in Japan, making many friends, admiring Japanese capacity, adaptability, generosity and intelligent curiosity, noting the beauty of simple things in everyday use, travelling by *rikisha* and train in many parts, and enjoying the national drama at the Imperial and other theatres in Tokyo, we determined to gratify a long-felt desire to pay a visit to Korea. Here are our experiences.

The traveller from Fusan to Seoul by the night train peers at daybreak through a double glass window from a well-equipped, comfortable, clean compartment at a landscape that cries out for those artist 'primitives' who were able to convey the beauty of low hills which owe nothing to foliage.

It was too early in spring for the blades of the rice plant to give more than a hint of greenness, and the rounded hills of Korea wove a spell, as does its ancient pottery. In the red dawn, as the train sped on, there were patches of soil that might well have been material for the potters of old ; mile upon mile of ancient soft greyness, patterned by rice fields round which paths like rabbit runs wound out and in. Here and there were groups of thatched dwellings that from the train looked more like overgrown mushrooms than homes for human beings.

As the day cleared, we saw dun-coloured bullocks wending their patient way with narrow, piled-high wagons ; others were hidden under giant loads of brushwood, their drivers trudging alongside or leading the way on foot. These men were tall, dignified figures, each with a straight, flat back, and coarse black hair dressed in a topknot. At every station were groups of countrymen, with or without hats, but all in white garments that in the distance suggested grave-clothes. There is luxury in the idea of white working garb, but heaven help the washerwomen ! The style of the garments is said to date back to the Chinese Ming period.

Then came glimpses of women and girls, wearing voluminous gauzy skirts and short bodices that were touched with brilliant blue, red or green. We had a feeling of pleasure in the bright colour and movement with that pastel background, while the morning sun turned the hilltops pink against deep shadows of velvety black.

From time to time groups of tall, white-clad men wearing the pyramidal native hat, not unlike the former headgear of Welsh women, clambered in and out of the train. Grotesque though this head-dress seemed at first, it presently assumed dignity. Perhaps all hats are

13

ridiculous ! Anyhow the serious expression of the Korean face disarmed our smiles. What fine fellows those men seemed ! They had slenderness, grace, tranquillity, but—they expectorated freely in Far Eastern fashion !

What a fuss human beings have always made about the dressing of their heads and their feet ! In the West a man's hair must be cropped hard to the skull. In the Far East a top-knot is, or used to be, a badge of manhood. As to footgear, the Korean seemed to have a slender and shapely foot. The women's feet are not bandaged as in old China, nor is the instep unbraced or broken by such footgear as the unyielding, flapping, picturesque *geta* of Japan. In place of sock or stocking, Koreans of both sexes wear a thick white cotton bootee with a seam up the instep. The foot is then pushed into a shoe, which is often made of a mosaic of paper, silk embroidery and leather. The shoes of both men and women seemed to be similar, with upward-curved toe, and they fitted neatly. A foreign friend once told me that when engaging a Korean domestic she judged her efficiency as a needlewoman by the neatness of the seams of her cotton bootees. The men's trousers were sometimes fastened at the ankle by coloured ribbon !

At every station on our long journey were groups of two, and sometimes more, armed Japanese soldiers in khaki uniform. A movement for national independence had been fermenting and there had been a national uprising on the day of the late Emperor's funeral,

 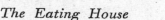 *See colour plate opposite*

The Eating House

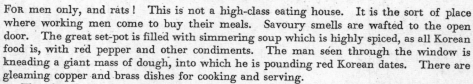

For men only, and rats ! This is not a high-class eating house. It is the sort of place where working men come to buy their meals. Savoury smells are wafted to the open door. The great set-pot is filled with simmering soup which is highly spiced, as all Korean food is, with red pepper and other condiments. The man seen through the window is kneading a giant mass of dough, into which he is pounding red Korean dates. There are gleaming copper and brass dishes for cooking and serving.

The place has great attraction, especially in cold weather, for countrymen who trudge long distances on foot and carry heavy baggage.

The thick vermicelli soup looks good as it bubbles gently. The vermicelli is made in long uncut strings and is eaten with a sort of gobble, much as Italians eat macaroni. The jars on the shelves hold various pickles and one great cauldron is full of boiling rice. The quality of Korean rice is such that many people prefer it to Chinese or Japanese. For the rest, there are dried fish, sliced pear, and the famous native cabbage pickle, called *kimchi*.

Koreans eat their food from beautiful brass bowls and have brass spoons. They also use chopsticks. At home it is bad manners to lift your bowl from the table, but in a restaurant manners are more free. Perhaps this is because women never eat in public places but always in the home.

The floor of this restaurant is of mud, pounded hard, and in dark corners and behind boxes rats lead a happy life. There are always clouds of flies buzzing over the eaters and their food, but however much the flies gorge they never take a nap as the men do, for after a good meal it is usual for a Korean man to have a nap—in his own room, or in the street, according to his way of life.

In one such small and dingy place as this establishment for working men the scroll over the doorway read, 'This eating-house is the best for seeing the moon !'

THE EATING HOUSE

but from the train window all seemed calm and mild as the face of a Korean woman gazing from its fur-trimmed hood.

Seoul, the capital of Korea (pronounced 'soul' or 'sowl' as you choose), lies in a saucer-like hollow and is set about by gently-sloping hills while thatched dwellings cluster thickly at the base of these hills. Like the New Jerusalem of St. John's vision, Seoul was at one time a walled city with beautiful gates. When I was there the ancient granite wall was crumbling to decay, but two of the massive stone gateways, with curving tiled roofs and high arches—wide enough for modern traffic—seemed good for hundreds of years. The gates are now open by day and by night. Against the Far Eastern background, I saw the spires of Western churches of different sects shooting up from various eminences. There were churches of Anglican and American Episcopalian, Presbyterian, Methodist, Roman Catholic and even Baptist and lesser sects, including the Salvation Army and Seventh Day Adventists. Some of the religious structures were flanked by mission schools, colleges and hospitals.

Seoul remains a memory of wide roads of yellow-grey granite, brilliant sunlight, intensely blue skies, long vistas, the wonderful gateways, and a constant stream of slow-moving oxen laden with brushwood. Leading the oxen there were always big, lean men in dusty cotton clothing and straw shoes that were noiseless in the golden dust. If one of them suffered the sad plight of being a bachelor in a Confucian land, his hair would be worn, not in a hard top-knot, but in a long queue and tied with a red ribbon. A newly engaged boy of ten or twelve may with impunity talk 'low talk' to a bachelor twice his age.

In April the gardens of Seoul were glowing with canary-coloured forsythia grouped near giant bushes of azalea of the sad, pale, lilac hue we associate with the old-fashioned rhodo-dendron. Greedy, noisy magpies were the bandits of the city, but flocks of swallows defied their impudence.

There were shops stacked with stiff horsehair men's hats in neatly-fitting cases. There were embroidered-shoe shops, the brass merchants' glowing shelves, and doorless shops for metal-bound cabinets and chests. There were windows showing amber and jade gewgaws, but most alluring of all, when its treasures were unlocked, was the store of the silk mercer.

There were many eating-houses—for men only—which sent forth savoury smells every hour of the day. Soup was boiled in great setpots. Other cooking operations went on in deep solid brass or copper basins over charcoal fires. Customers thronged in and out of the open doors. Wise-eyed, plump rats did their share of ridding the earthen floors of crumbs and juicy droppings, but thick clouds of flies had ever the best of the feast. Korean food is rich and varied, but it is so highly peppered with the native red pepper—great beautiful bunches of which were always in evidence—that one mouthful would make the foreigner weep. Strange pickles, and especially the native *kimchi*, a cabbage pickled with red pepper and other hot condiments, were helped from glorious, smooth, honey-coloured jars, and bowls of rare blue held unknown flavours.

At many doorways there were the inevitable lazy men, smoking long pipes and gazing into dreamland.

There was everywhere the rare charm of the native costume. The material might be of silk, grasscloth or cotton. Flour sacks were often ripped by thrifty Koreans and, when washed and pounded, according to ancient Korean laundry usage, were used for making men's pants and other hard-wearing garments. The men's coats were long and narrow, their trousers baggy and wide.

The dress of the children was of the same pattern and style as that of their parents and grandparents, but the colours were more varied.   Little girls had generally wide rose-pink skirts reaching to their ankles ; small boys often had coats of the same colour.   The boys' white trousers, like those of the men, were baggy and of ankle length.   Infants' short jackets had rainbow-striped sleeves.   The effect of the dress of old and young under an azure sky against a background of grey stone and whitewashed walls made a gratifying colour scheme.

A nation of white-robed and white-trousered Korean males naturally means a nation of laundering females.   In China and in Japan men are the washboys, but in Korea only women soak and rub and pound and toil at the gossamer clothing of old and young.   Turn where one might in Korea, at every stream, creek and runnel were to be seen groups of women and small girls battering the family linen.   They used paddles which they beat against the clothes on smooth stones in running water.   Women would go far upstream to get clear water for their washing.   In winter they would even sit on the edge of an icehole to rinse their family linen in the running water below.

Before the clothes were laundered each garment had been ripped up the seams to make it easy to iron the material on the special Korean ironing block.   Washing was important, but Korean ironing was still more exacting of human labour.   The sound in Seoul of women ironing was of an insistent beating of hard wooden sticks on muffled metal, wood, or stone.   This rhythmic clink began at early dawn and was sometimes to be heard far into the night.   Cloth so pounded gets a new texture.   The coarsest cotton gains a glossy sheen, while fine materials become like gauze.   Alas ! constant ironing means swollen wrists and sometimes dislocated thumbs for the ironer.

At first it was something of a puzzle to guess why, at so many turns of the streets of Seoul, long narrow strips of brightly-coloured material seemed to be ever billowing in the breeze.   Very often the strips were of a beautiful rosy pink, but some were blue, some green and some yellow.   These were lengths of cotton or silk, carefully re-dyed on being laundered at home.   Formerly the dyes came always from China, and were vegetable, not chemical, dyes ; hence their beauty.

The traveller of 1919, who kept to the broad thoroughfares and travelled by street car, might find parts of Seoul as dull and ugly as other partly-Westernised cities of the Far East, but let him enter some of the winding, narrow alleys and he would have peeps of mysterious courtyard interiors with tall Aladdin-like jars ;   or through a whitewashed stone archway he would be sure to see a group of tousled black-haired children in bright clothes dancing and playing in the sunlight.   Beyond their lively figures, outside the open door of the courtyard, there would be stacked more of the black-brown pickle jars and many glossy yellow gourds.   Every turn of every alley would reveal new pictures.

In a small room scarcely six feet square I remember seeing two old men with faces like those of sages on an ancient Chinese scroll.   Their clothing was a mellow white.   On their heads were small close-fitting transparencies, worn indoors to cover their top-knots.   One of the men, facing the opening, was smoking contemplatively a long-stemmed pipe, the bowl of which touched the floor while he listened to his friend, an aged man with shoulders bowed, who was reading aloud in a quavering voice from a faded scroll of the ancient classics.

The nature of the reading might well have been something like the following as translated by Dr. Gale :

'Where is God that He can hear so well ?   So vast is the universe, I wonder !   Still, when I come to think of it, it is not a question of height or of distance, God is in the heart.

'Secret words that men whisper to one another God hears as a clap of thunder ;   and the dark designs plotted within the inner chamber, he sees as a flash of lightning.

KITE-FLYING

'When a man's measure of wickedness is full, God takes him away.

'When a man through wrong-doing wins great renown, do not be disturbed about it, for if he is not killed by his fellow men, God will see to it.

'When you sow cucumbers, you reap cucumbers ; when you sow beans you reap beans.   The meshes of God's fishing net seem very wide indeed, yet none of us shall ever escape through them.

'Life and death are ordered by God, as also are riches and poverty.

'God never made a man without supplying his need.

'The hidden wickedness of the heart is what we need to fear, for God's eyes, like wheels, turn— seeing everything.'

See preceding colour plate

Kite-Flying

SEOUL, the capital, is an ideal place for kite-flying, and suddenly one day when the season arrives you wake to find the sky full of gay kites.   For days the shops, even the smallest— and the smallest shops in the world seem to be in Korea—had been full of gaily-coloured kites, some of them as cheap as a penny.

This is a typical group of children, kite-flying against the background of the old city wall which winds up and down the hillside—to-day, alas, with many breaks and gaps.   As the hills round Seoul are not too steep even for boys and girls to climb, it is an ideal spot for this fascinating game, and nowhere are there more daring and skilful fliers.

Strange accidents happen to kites.   Korean paper is tough and strong but some kites get hung up on trees and stay there until they become tattered shreds, fluttering in the branches like ghosts for many weeks.   Even rain and violent March winds do not destroy kites quickly.

At the New Year, grown-ups have contests in kite-flying.   The object is to cut the rival's strings.   This is done by rubbing the string with ground glass and porcelain mixed with glue.   Dr. Gale in his *Korean Sketches* says that he considers these kite-flying contests are as exciting as anything to be seen on an American baseball field.

B

Chapter Two   ✿   The Scholar

WE were fortunate in having a friend to greet us in Seoul, the late Dr. James S. Gale, who for more than thirty years had been among the foremost literary interpreters to the West of the Korean mind. It may be that no one ever knew Korea better, or loved her people more understandingly. Travellers, artists, students, archæologists, journalists and literary folk, officials and diplomats, who went to China by way of Seoul, inevitably carried in their wallets letters of introduction to this able and clear-eyed Canadian scholar-missionary.

Denying ourselves the luxury of the palatial, Western-style Government hotel in Seoul, of which the Japanese were so proud, we were fortunate enough to be received at the American Methodist Medical Mission, where we boarded during the whole of our stay in the Peninsula. As we had come to Seoul to make a study of the Korean people, we wished to live among foreigners who knew and valued them. Each day with this kindly background, we hoped to be able to follow, consciously and unconsciously, the pattern of Korean daily life.

The head of the Mission Hospital was a woman doctor, Mary Stuart, a patriotic native of Kansas, who was sure that the food, clothing, teaching, and missioning among the heathen, everything indeed that came from the Land of the Free, was the best in the world. The doctor was a rare character and had some prejudices, but she had also courage, industry and deep religious feeling, and she was bigger than her creed. On the table of her sitting-room her Bible lay open at a passage in Romans which was her daily guide.

After a day or two the doctor told us that when Dr. Gale brought us to see her, she and her staff had reason to be a little suspicious. A story had gone the round of the foreign community that 'the two English ladies were spies'! The doctor told us that she had tossed her head at this, and vowed that she was not in the least afraid, and that if we were spies it was so much the worse for us. Soon the talk of spies became a Mission joke, and we were being trusted with every story that came to the hospital of Korean suffering before and since the uprising of March 1, and of Japanese pigheadedness and cruelty in their treatment of the Korean people.

Every night after supper the doctor would rest by her smokeless-fuel fire while she poured into my willing ear moving experiences that explained her devotion to the Koreans among whom she worked.

The doctor believed in a good table. British apple pie is good, but Kansas apple pie was a compound of apple infiltrated with cream, set within a fairy-like puff and served with whipped cream to a point of perfection.   The doctor's before-meal grace was a brief but pointed counsel to the Almighty : 'Bless us this day, O Lord ! Bless this food to our eating, and bless all those who have no food this day !'

As Britishers who had not at that time visited America, we knew nothing of American Methodists, their missions, aims, aspirations or personnel, but we never ceased to be grateful for the introduction to this group.   The spirit of the place was free, kindly and hard-working. It was taken for granted that I should tap out my impressions on my typewriter at any hour of the day, and that my artist sister, accompanied by a native youth who helped to carry the sketching materials and held a big Korean parasol to shield the artist from the sun, should start off early every morning to find subjects.   The youth, who looked a stolid, unemotional type and rarely aired his English, was in reality one of the many Korean heroes.   Carried in the hidden fold of the tie that fastened his cotton coat was 'copy' for the secret Korean *Independence News* or some other incriminating piece of writing.   This we discovered long afterwards.

The foreign-style, red-brick buildings of the Mission were grouped on the steep, sunny hillside, just within the ancient, beautiful East Gate of Seoul.   The largest of the group was the hospital for women which stood on the shoulder of the hillside, while, down at the bottom, was the woefully small dispensary where a stream of sick and sorry humanity was treated daily by the clever doctor and a young Korean girl who had been trained in Japan.   A tall Swedish-American was head of the nursing department, and was able, devoted and highly intelligent with an overflowing fund of humour and good temper.

Life at the hospital had its amusing side, but during that spring in Seoul the general atmosphere was tense and tragic.   Up the valley they came, the anæmic, the tubercular, sometimes those suffering from what the Japanese call 'the shameful disease,' sometimes victims of parasites, and mothers and babies who had survived the experimental physicking of the witch-doctor ;   women with aching teeth or lacquer poisoning, and an occasional sufferer from chastisement by an old-fashioned husband disappointed in not having children or in having girls only.   There were patients with sore eyes, crippled toes, broken limbs and skin diseases and, apparently without ceasing, a continuous arrival of expectant mothers.

It was hard to believe that so much suffering was hidden under the dainty native dress. The women's gowns, home-dyed and hand-stitched, were of cotton, grasscloth, silk or brocade. They might be white or a delicate blue-green.   The ribbons that tied the short bodices were crimson, and the silk cuffs that edged the long narrow sleeves, royal blue.   A glance at the women's dress revealed to the initiated whether they were mothers-in-law, young wives or 'concubines'.   All the women had sleek, black heads.   Their hair, parted in the centre and smoothly drawn back into a massive knot at the nape of the neck, was ornamented by a broad, red ribbon or by heavy silver or jade pins.   As the days grew warmer, the women's skirts became more and more diaphanous, and great balloon-like trousers reaching to the ankles showed plainly.

The Korean women are small-boned, and their faces have a gentle expression.   Patient submission would seem to have become second nature.   But try to guide these meek-seeming females in a new direction, fail to yield to some deep-rooted prejudice or belief, and the hills that circle the city of Seoul may be as easily moved.   There are many ways to their warm hearts, but the way to their wills is learned only through patient kindness with due regard to Korean custom.

When you are told that most Oriental women endure the pangs of childbirth without uttering a cry, you must resist the hasty conclusion that they have escaped the curse of Eve, or that they have no quarrel with the limitations of their lot.   If they must suffer childbirth with groanings that cannot be uttered, they earn the right to water their couch with tears by reason of their afflictions at the hands of their native healers.

One day a woman was brought to East Gate Hospital suffering from poisoned wounds. Her friend explained to the doctor that when the woman had had her previous baby she had been badly torn.   It was said further that her attendants had burnt the torn places because they did not mend.   They kept on burning at intervals and yet she got worse !   They then called in the sorceress, who gave the patient water to drink in which tigers' teeth and claws had been boiled.   The sorceress also blew her horn, shook her red rags, jangled her bells, and danced with generous abandon, but the evil spirit was not thus to be quenched.   As a last hope they had brought the patient to the hospital to try the foreigner's magic.   After some weeks of careful nursing, the young mother, with her baby, was sent home perfectly well.

Besides the custom of burning wounds, there is the well-known use of the 'needle', which the native doctor pushes into any part of the body where pain may lurk.   At times the pain of the needle-thrust helps the patient to forget the original pain.   Some sturdy patients survive, but occasionally the needle-thrusting sends them where we hope they will feel pain no more.

See colour plate opposite

Woman Sewing

HERE is a middle-class Korean woman sewing, with her sewing-box by her side, and near it her brass charcoal holder ready to heat the metal ironing rod for pressing seams.   The women have a high standard in their ironing methods and any garments they launder seem to be of the finest texture with a gossamer sheen.

The servant is busy in the kitchen department, the drawback to which, from a Western angle, is that the rooms are enclosed by a dead wall and therefore there is no view.   The stone floors are covered with the familiar oiled yellow waxed paper which gets a beautiful sheen with constant rubbing, and the floors are warm by reason of the smoke from the kitchen flues passing under them.

The thimble which the Korean lady uses is like a tiny tea-cosy and is beautifully embroidered with coloured silks.   It adds a charming finishing touch to the delicate style of the women's dress.

The lady is sitting in the women's side of the house.   The ceiling is low as always in Korean rooms, and the small room is crowded with tall, flat-faced, beautiful Korean chests, some of polished wood, others of red lacquer and all bound with brass hinges and handles and other interesting ornamentation.   These tall, flat-faced, brass-bound Korean chests have long been famous, but to understand their great usefulness they should be seen in use by a Korean lady.   The lady in the picture took out various garments which she had made for sale to help the poor, and it was a marvel to see how much the chest held, all in perfect order.   No woman would search with unseemly haste for a misplaced garment, yet each chest is packed to its utmost capacity.   Such order speaks of centuries of restraint. The chest is the chief, indeed the only, furniture except for tiny dining or tea tables. Perhaps the most beautiful of all the chests were the black lacquered ones inlaid with mother-of-pearl, of a delicacy of workmanship that it would be difficult to over-praise.

WOMAN SEWING

A patient arrived one day suffering from lock-jaw. The native doctor had pushed needles into the woman's jaw and into the soles of her feet, but the jaw had stayed locked ! An aged crone suggested that the woman be taken to East Gate Hospital, for, she assured her gossips, the foreign doctor there was a worker of miracles. The old dame herself led the way—a distance of some twenty miles on foot from the village.

The doctor had a beautiful flexible hand, and when she had examined the woman's mouth and had deftly inserted her forefinger, she unlocked the jaw. The amazement of the patient and her friends was unbounded. 'There ! Did I not tell you ?' exclaimed the old dame. 'Always obey her, for she can cure just like Jesus did !'

In Confucian Korea where ancestor worship is a stubborn tradition, generation is the great social fact. Marriage is often arranged between minors, and child-bearing begins at seventeen and sometimes earlier. The great dread in a family is that it may die out, and the women are as eager to do their part to prevent this as the menfolk could wish. The doctor told the story of a woman who had had twelve children, all of whom had died at birth. The family group were against further experiment, but the woman herself was obdurate. As a final hope, when her next baby was due, her mother-in-law and a friend brought her to the Mission Hospital. The doctor delivered the child safely, and the mother, under an anæsthetic, knew nothing until she awoke to the bliss of holding her baby. Four days later the patient was found trying to escape from the hospital, she was in such haste to get home to show her precious baby to the family, though it was only a girl !

Some of the doctor's sayings come back to mind. 'Yes,' she said, 'some folks say the Koreans are lazy, but I say laziness has a cause. In this country it's worms. I took a big tape-worm out of one woman, and more than two hundred hook-worms out of another woman. What ails these poor folks is underfeeding and worms !'

Before Japan laid her conquering hand on Korea the influence of the Christian missionary was well-established. He found in the Korean a simple, unspoilt mind with a traditional reverence for scholarship, and a deep-rooted contempt for military power. No better authority can be quoted on this subject than Dr. Gale, who said on a memorable occasion to a group of Japanese officials who had come to consult him :

'The Korean lives apart in a world of wonder, something quite unlike our modern civilisation, in a beautiful world of the mind. I have studied for thirty years to enter sympathetically into this world of the Korean mind and I am still an outsider. Yet the more I penetrate this ancient Korean civilisation the more I respect it.'

Dr. Gale writes further on the subject of Korean acceptance of Christian teaching :

'The East and the Far East have generally had a poor reception for missionaries from the West because of the general inability of the masses to read the Bible. This applies to the Nearer East and India, with their complicated forms of writing.

'Perhaps China was worst of all as she sailed along complacently on her literary ideals, while her poor and unlettered ones have had to live on the bones of rumour, hearsay and superstition. *In the Far East, Korea has been the one great exception by virtue of her simple and efficient script.*

'Korea, by what prophetic instinct we know not, prepared 460 years ago, a simple form of writing so that the old and poor, the toilworn, the prisoner, the baker, the hat-mender, the water-carrier, the bean-curd pedlar, the witch wife, the less-than-no-man—all might read. To-day, among successful Korean church workers are those who never had a day's schooling in their lives. King Se-Jong's simple alphabet has served as a medium for the transmission of the Scriptures, and the land of the

Hermit has been put in touch with all the familiar Bible stories clear down from Eden to the Sea of Galilee.

'Also, Korea has prepared a way by her special name for God—*Hananim*—by the attributes ascribed to him, by the associations of everyday life, by the place accorded to literature and by their easy and comprehensive writing.

'*The Chinese and Japanese have no such concept of the one God.*'

It is generally admitted also that the Koreans are the best linguists in the Far East. Koreans who have never been out of their own country often speak Japanese so well that it is difficult to tell whether they are Japanese or Korean.

Korea is the only 'heathen' country converted to Christianity that has sent missionaries to other lands. It is said that the Chinese more readily accept Christianity from Koreans than from any Western teacher. There is even a story of a Korean preacher being chosen by a group of hard-headed Nova Scotians to be their pastor.

Whereas China got from the West trade, mechanics, shipping, railroads and factories, with Christianity as an antidote, the Koreans imported a somewhat crude evangelical Christianity and continued trading with their Far Eastern neighbours as before.

Some readers may have a conscious, or perhaps unconscious, prejudice against the word 'missionary', but no open-minded traveller in Korea could fail to appreciate the astonishing modernising influence of the Christian missionary in that country.

The Korean scholar had always been honoured as a prince even when his clothes were in tatters, so the journeyings of St. Paul and the Apostles were stories the Korean people easily understood.

Chapter Three The Sorceress and the Priestess

APICTURE of Korea, its soul struggles, undaunted courage, self-control, power of endurance in danger and oppression, and eagerness to learn—qualities found alike in young men and women of the student groups and even among intelligent children, as proved by the courage of girls and boys of twelve and even younger, who helped in the dangerous work of producing and delivering the secret *Independence News*—would be incomplete if the writer were to ignore the survival of ancient superstious beliefs.

A charming American girl who spoke Korean was eager to join me in viewing a Sorceress dance.

My companion and I set off early one beautiful spring morning for the sorceress's dwelling which stood high on the slope of a romantic valley outside the crumbling walls of ancient Seoul. Nothing more unlike the hags of Shakespeare could have been pictured than the prosperous, friendly, smiling being who welcomed us on the morning of her occult performance. It was clear that she had never heard the ominous command, 'Thou shalt not suffer a witch to live !'

As we climbed the slope my companion and I could speak of nothing but the beauty of the valley. A May breeze stirred the spray of green willows that grew on both sides of the stream. The wide road of broken granite led upwards towards the rocks and pines of the hills which were bathed in the gold of early sunlight. Two hawks were circling high overhead, the only creatures in sight, but we could hear the monotonous thud where, hidden by a bend of the river, women were beating the family linen on boulders in the flowing water.

How was it that the whole scene became suddenly old, old ? Ah ! There it was ! The sound of the witch's primeval orchestra—pink-punka-punk-pink ! Pink-punka-punk-pink ! beat a flat-toned drum, and a thinner-toned drum seemed to respond unceasingly, tumpta-tumpta-tum-tum !

Suddenly, both the drumming and the dancing stopped. As we turned the corner to the house we saw that the company had paused to rest and have a smoke. The whole side of the witch's dwelling, encircled by a white-washed mud wall, was open to the day. The large room where the dancing and drumming had been going on was low-ceiled. Its floor was covered by the usual shiny, Korean yellow waxed paper, and dwarf tables were set along the back wall of the room. On these, many coloured cakes and fruit, and a variety of strange foods, were massed on plates and in gleaming brass bowls. There were also decorations of tawdry, waxen paper flowers. Over all the flies buzzed in clouds.

Three apartments were visible besides the big room. In one, on the left, three young married women, all smoking, knelt in consultation. Another room adjoining was the witch's kitchen. It had a divided door, reminiscent of Ireland, the upper half of which was open. Within could be seen a pretty young girl, wearing a pink bodice and a dark cotton skirt. Her black glossy hair caught the light, and her newly-powdered face had a flower-like pallor. For the rest the kitchen was shadowed in steam and smoke. The girl was bending forward in absorbed attention while she stirred a huge cauldron of savoury-smelling stew or broth for the midday meal. Through the open window in a far wall of the kitchen, blue skies and green trees at the other side of the valley gleamed relief. The room on the right of the big apartment had a square hole in the partition wall, and through this opening there peered the bovine face of a girl of perhaps fourteen.

There were about a dozen women in the big room, besides the dancer. Four of these were musicians, all seemingly blind. There were two males present—a youth with tousled hair and dirty white clothing, who poised a pair of cymbals ready to clash at a given signal, and an older man who played a kind of flute. A few of the old women were merely sympathetic and neighbourly. None had duties but the aged dame who waited on the sorceress.

See colour plate opposite

The Bride

THE most tragic figure of old Korea! On her wedding day she must not move, look or eat. Formerly even her eyes were pasted down with rice paper. She is carried to her place of honour, for her feet must not touch the earth. Her face is coloured white but with two spots of red painted on the cheeks and one on the forehead. Her lips also are reddened. At feasting time, while everyone else is sharing in the good things, a table piled with tempting food is placed before her, but she must not eat. Sometimes a little fruit juice is carefully squeezed inside her mouth, but the lips must not be smeared. All day long she sits on the women's side of the house, blind and dumb like an image while all around her there is a flow of compliments and criticisms.

The Bride's mother has also a strenuous day waiting on her guests without time to share in the feast. For the Bridegroom, on the contrary, it is a glorious day of feasting and entertaining his friends in a separate apartment.

In old-fashioned families it used to be considered a disgrace if a girl was not married before she was twenty. It was also considered a disgrace—unless there was a very special reason—for a widow to remarry. Tradition was strong, but to-day these old prejudices and ancient family customs have changed or are speedily changing.

There are some brides with modern education who rebel against the old customs. One bride who had been well-educated and could speak English was married into an old-fashioned family. The girl was proud and strong-willed and refused to wait while the family were having meals. Her father-in-law tried to break her spirit but was defeated. Her baby died and the young mother defied all tradition and left the house. A new spirit is speedily changing all the bad old social customs and the young men are as eager as the young women to follow in modern ways.

THE BRIDE

The women wore the usual airy voluminous skirts and short bodices. Their black hair was parted and drawn tightly back at the nape of the neck where it was caught by heavy ornamental pins. Their shaven foreheads gave a momentary impression of intellectuality, but soft dark eyes relieved the severity of line, and the whole effect was sweet and calm.

The sorceress, a woman over fifty, pockmarked and stout, with genial, laughing mouth and clever eyes, was squatting in the centre of the room smoking a long pipe, which her aged, wrinkled attendant filled and lit for her. Close to her sat the lady on whose behalf the spirits were being invoked. She was bravely dressed for the ceremony in rich blue brocade, and the classic hairdressing made plain the gaunt outline of her narrow-built head and lean neck. She was restless and her voice was full of woe. The sorceress talked much with her in a soothing tone, occasionally pausing to emphasise her words with many a motherly pat.

Presently the sorceress handed her pipe to the attendant and rose to her feet. She was helped into elegant dancing gowns. First, a blue silk skirt was wound round her waist, next came a short wide coat lined with an enthralling shade of vivid blue with an outer covering of gauzy material of a faded golden brown, the interwoven design merging into a warmer shade of colour. The garments were of antique cut suggesting Chinese influence.

The dancer was fat and broadly built, but her feet were small, and their shapely slimness was enhanced by perfectly-fitting thick, white cotton heel-less boots. Her wide trousers showed in wrinkled folds around her ankles. As the dancer rose slowly the cymbals clashed and one drum beat. The dancer moved with grace, dancing always on the flat of her foot in time to the beating of the drum, meanwhile chanting in a nasal tone. First she bowed, bringing her hands together till the papers merged. Then she turned to the tables of food and bowed, the drums and cymbals punctuating each movement. Now the drum beating increased in speed, the other drums joined in, and the dancer moved faster and faster, waving the papers over her right and left shoulders alternately as her chanting grew louder.

The aged attendant handed the dancer a little brass rattle with half a dozen bells attached and a large, tattered fan, and threw over her left arm a long streamer of yellow silk. The priestess danced and intoned in rhythm with the drumming and clashing of the musicians, and, as she danced, the paper streamers, the silk, the rattle and the fan played their part. Her body swayed now this way, now that, and her small white feet seemed to hold the secret of perfect time. At intervals the dancer would bring the flat of one foot down with a hard thud on the floor, like the pounding of a hare. From swaying and rising up and down she next began to twirl round and round, and although her voice got breathy she never stopped chanting. The beating, clashing and intoning acted like a spell, and her body seemed to move hypnotically. Twice during the dance she moved to the entrance and followed the practice of a queen of ancient Ireland who despised pocket handkerchiefs, but she resumed the dance so quickly that it was hard to realise that a break had been made.

It was a strange scene for that sunny spring morning—the low-ceiled room, the flyblown viands, the gaudy decorations, the squatting women, the strenuous blind musicians, and the swirling central figure. One aged crone with watchful bright eyes and immobile figure, smoked throughout the proceedings, while another old woman, wrinkled and toothless, slumbered against a wall. The younger women watched intently every turn of the dance, and often joined in the chanting, making a sort of wild chorus. In the tiny inner room the three smoking young women never glanced at the dancer but smoked throughout the din.

Of the musicians, a very small woman beat the biggest drum. Her staring dark eyes suggested blindness, and, after watching for a time, I found that the protruding eyes of the untidy youth who clashed his cymbals with zeal and precision, were also sightless. Another drummer was a thin, tall woman, in a pale blue and white spotlessly neat gown. Throughout the whole of the drum-beating a cluster of flies, unmolested, stuck fast to her high white forehead. The young girl whose face and head filled the open square in the partition wall kept on staring at the scene like a spell-bound heifer, while the kitchen half-door space revealed always the pale-faced pretty young cook with the pink bodice, either stirring or ladling broth, and ever through the cloud of steam the far-off peaceful landscape gleamed.

Varying groups of children gathered in the little courtyard to watch the performance. The small boys wore soiled white clothing, and their rough black hair was tied in long queues. The small girls—small-boned maidens—wore long skirts of rose-pink cotton.

The sound of the chanting voices rose and fell, now reaching a shrill high note, again falling drowsily into a deep-toned refrain while the pump, pump of the drums encircled and enclosed all minor sounds, and seemed inseparable from the mesmerism of the dance as were the clouds of flies that buzzed and quivered on food, floor, walls, faces—on everything, animate and inanimate.

The sorceress's dancing and wailing seemed to lure into consciousness strange feelings of ancient times where slumbered human beliefs too remote for the historian. Emotions were stirred as if a memory of pain long abated were pressing on the unwilling fancy.

The priestess addressed her client in a nasal chant. The little woman, with bent head, responded in a similar key. As the questioning and responses went on, tears gathered in the eyes of the devotee, and the expression of her face was full of pain, but she seemed to have implicit faith in her motherly priestess. The tears got bigger and presently welled over, but the patient rubbed her rough palms and continued the response. Presently the enchantress stopped intoning, the cymbals ceased ; only the pale-faced drummer, with the flies still clustering on her forehead, kept up an independent thin tattoo.

The stout figure of the dancer slowed down gradually to a light floating movement. Then the dancing and singing ceased ; the cymbals and the big drum stopped. The anxious old servant disrobed the priestess, who renewed her questioning, and, unconscious of fatigue, did not even mop her moist, pock-marked forehead. The glowing coat and bright skirt were reverently folded, and the good-tempered face of the priestess beamed on the little woman with the blue bodice while she glided to the floor, and taking her patient's hands in her own, gave them sundry affectionate pats.

The aged attendant now handed the priestess a small black bowl of wood or metal in which were counters, and my companion whispered to me that the lady with the blue bodice was not suffering from illness but from 'family trouble', and the enchantress was now going to read her fortune. When the fortune-reading was over, the sorceress invited us to stay longer while she rested, as later, she assured us, there was to be dancing of a more ecstatic kind. We thanked her warmly but had to go.

At this moment two uniformed men arrived, the inevitable Japanese officials, who evidently wanted to know what two foreigners were doing at the house. The sorceress gave them one of her motherly smiles and a graceful bow, and, after consultation with each other, both officials left.

The company pressed to the opening to give us a kind send-off, and our last glimpse of the plaintive-faced lady in the blue silk bodice showed her full of trust as ever in the power

THE HAT SHOP

of her stout friend to lay the skeleton in her family cupboard. That kindly dame was now spreading out the white counters and seemed once more to concentrate her whole intelligence on the job in hand.

As we turned homeward, the valley was brilliant in the full morning sun. The near hills were in shadow but for one far peak like a snowy cloud in the sky, which seemed to merge into some kingdom in the heavens.

*   *   *

Old Tong See, the Buddhist priestess, was one of the picturesque figures at the Mission. Some share of the small shrine at which Tong See used daily to minister belonged to her, and her income was partly got in cash and partly in goods offered at the shrine by worshippers.

In Korea, dwelling houses rarely have chimneys. As in ancient Rome, domestic fires are lit either in a hollow scooped out under ground level, or in an outside wall of the dwelling, the smoke of the fire escaping under the flooring to the other side of the house. The system has merit in a cold country like Korea, but great care must be taken that the flames are neither too big nor too fierce.

One cold March day the floor of Tong See's shrine caught fire, and the priestess, who was bending over a table arranging sacrificial offerings, fell through the burning floor and badly injured her feet and legs.

The American doctor was brought to see the suffering woman. She dressed the wounds and bandaged her in comfortable soft wrappings, but the burns were serious and the doctor persuaded the people at the shrine to allow the patient to be moved to the foreign hospital where she could be properly nursed. After some weeks of medical care, Tong See's wounds were healed.

While Tong See lay in the ward in her white bed, she overheard the daily Christian reading, singing and praying that took place there, but as she was a Buddhist and a priestess at that, no one spoke to her on the subject of religion.

Tong See was a general favourite, and when she said good-bye to the doctor and her staff she expressed very grateful thanks. About a month later the old woman returned to the hospital and told the doctor that she had sold her Buddhist robes, had disposed of her share in the shrine, had indeed arranged all her worldly affairs and had made up her mind to live at the hospital and become a Christian.

The doctor explained to Tong See that the hospital was 'a place for sick folks and nurses', and that there was no room for her there, but the nurses pleaded Tong See's cause so eloquently that the doctor gave in. Tong See brought her mattress, which she spread in the hallway every night in a screened corner, and this temporary sleeping-place had remained her bedroom ever since.

The old lady learnt to read and went regularly to a class to study the Bible. She never tired of telling her Buddhist friends about the joys of the Christian life. The happy expression of Tong See's wrinkled, kind old face was better than any sermon.

It is such a story that brings to mind the missionary literature of one's childhood and the sense of discomfort that some Sunday School talks used to leave on the mind. British, and especially Scottish, people rarely speak of spiritual experiences. Yet to the devoted men and women who go to foreign lands with the grand aspiration of helping so-called 'heathen' people, their simple gospel phraseology becomes natural. One wonders what a 'converted'

Far Easterner, man or woman, thinks when visiting the West to find that the language they have come to associate with Western idealists is not in everyday use in their home lands !

Pondering often on some such problems while staying at this mission centre, I was awakened very early one lovely summer morning by the sound of exquisite fluting. Soon it came to me that I was listening for the first time to that pure-throated fountain of delight, the golden oriole. On other mornings when no oriole roused me, I used to be wakened by the harsh tones of a Korean Christian, and from my window I could see a man in native dress with hat complete, bowing to the rising sun, hands clasped, singing lustily a Christian hymn in Korean to a Sankey and Moody air !

See preceding colour plate

The Hat Shop

'TALL hat, round hat, ribbon and every kind of hat from every possible quarter of the globe' says the sign, I am told. The hat shop is very small, and, as you see, the hat seller is very big, but he always makes room for another tall friend or even several tall friends and there they seem to sit smoking and chatting all day long.

If a gentleman buys a hat for a friend, he will either buy one of the coloured cases to hold it or he will put it on top of his own hat. Sometimes a man will wear several hats on his head in this fashion. All the hive-shaped cases in the shop are hat-boxes.

Hats are important. Scholars wear a special shape of hat or cap of black horsehair. None but those who are learned in Chinese classics may wear such a hat.

The engaged boy wears a circular hat of yellow straw. At a wedding one man wears a red hat hired for the occasion. He carries the wedding goose. All these old customs are changing and to-day Korean men, young and old, are wearing ugly modern felt hats just like other men.

The yellow, paper-covered, cone-shaped boxes outside the shop are the cases for carrying the precious hats a long distance ; I often spied them in houses while sketching their owners.

Chapter Four   ❧   The Nobleman

THERE was a group of fine peonies in their prime—white, pink and a deep, glowing crimson. For the rest the garden was all greenness except for a budding cream magnolia. Although in no sense a rock garden, there were many big stones, some of them ancient and carved, dividing the paths. There was a shady nook on the slope on which, under a gnarled old pine, was a reclining couch of stone covered by a blanket, and seats near, so that the host and his guests might sit and smoke and write Chinese poems. The garden was small as we count gardens in the West, but it was full of suggestion.

There were scenes and vistas and little winding paths. One led to a knoll covered by flowering shrubs, where a fine view could be had of beautiful Seoul and far-stretching valleys. Another path, covered by thick trees, led to a little natural grotto where in the cleft of a rock was a spring. Here the old gentleman could sit and meditate. Here he might bathe in perfect seclusion.

The heavy tiled roof of the dwelling facing the garden where guests were received was covered by a thick wistaria massed with bright green leaves that trailed in long heavy branches to the outer veranda. This little house had three small rooms where guests were formally received. A reception room in the Far East seems bare to Western eyes, but the proportions are good and there are no small distracting objects nor cumbrous furniture. In the rooms we entered the floors were covered with the national honey-coloured waxed paper, polished and shining by constant rubbing and use.

The first room held an eight-fold screen with fine old painted panels. The kneeling cushions were covered in silk embroidery of antique design. The three apartments were connected by paper covered doors. There were elbow rests to match the small tables which were used for holding teacups or writing materials. On other small tables were long-stemmed Korean pipes with tiny brass bowls. The interior had simplicity and dignity.

Two sons whom we knew came to greet us. One of them spoke English well. Both boys were slender and had high-bred faces. They wore long white cotton coats, but their shoes and socks were Western style. The old gentleman had Korean footgear.

The interior of the reception house had little to suggest the family's distinguished past except a few framed photographs of our host when he had held a high Court position. One picture with a gilt frame was veiled by a cover of red silk. The veil was removed later to show us a photograph of the late Emperor.

The old gentleman gave an order and one of the sons disappeared, returning with a tea tray, and we knelt and sipped while our friend the American doctor chatted with the family in Korean. Soon a daughter-in-law joined us. This was a privilege, as Korean ladies rarely meet casual guests.

It was hard to believe, on this bright sunny day, in this snug corner surrounded by glowing roses and early summer greenery, that tragedy was shadowing the country and falling heavily on this family. So far they had all escaped prison, but it was rare that a Japanese detective was absent, and the old Viscount was virtually a prisoner.

Not a word was said of the present political situation. We chatted pleasantly of travel, flowers and pictures. We heard about different members of the family. The eldest son— husband of the daughter-in-law—was in Europe, but he was spoken of happily although we all knew that he could never return to his native land under the present regime. This young man had not been guilty of any offence, nor had he opposed the Government, but as a member of a high family he was held to be dangerous.

This exiled son had had great difficulty in getting abroad. The Government had put innumerable obstacles in his way but, skilfully, he had got out of the country without a passport. He could never return, nor could his young wife get leave to join him.

The daughter-in-law had a beautiful face. Her dark hair was dressed in smooth Korean style, knotted at the nape of the neck and tied with red ribbon. Her gown was of plain white cotton. A Korean woman holds her shoulders flat and her head high.

Presently our host gave the word and we were led along the outer veranda towards the back of the house. We found ourselves in a little covered way leading to another veranda which surrounded the women's quarters. Several of the odd Korean nests for domestic poultry were slung from poles at the end of one small house. These nests are like small straw hammocks, and here the fowls retire in dignity when they would oblige the family.

Like the men's reception rooms the whole of the women's and servants' quarters were in one storey and all had the same floor-covering of yellow paper. All rooms seemed to open into each other.

There was one small square room that was packed with fine old Korean brass-bound cabinets reaching to the ceiling. As there were reclining mattresses on the floor it was probably a bedroom. One mattress, covered by pale green silk brocade, was raised on a frame of dark polished wood. Our host seated himself on this, waving us to flat, silk-covered kneeling cushions. The sons apologised for the absence of their mother, and the daughter-in-law acted as hostess.

The boys, again on their father's order, fetched some old family pictures which were unrolled for our entertainment. One was beautiful. It was about three yards long and gave a panoramic view in colour of ancient Korea. They called it a 'dream' picture. Three hundred years before an artist had painted it from a description of a poet's dream. The picture, mellow with age, was a delicate drawing on silk, giving consecutive peeps of old Korea, or, shall we say, of a poet's old Korea, for it was a sublimated land that the painter had skilfully placed on silk. It held the quality of romance inseparable from hills and trees in the Far East, and each scene as the picture was unrolled, was linked in perfect continuity. The onlooker might have been sitting on a cloud watching the old world of the Far East roll slowly by. The tiny figures of Korean men of old were limned in incomparable blues and reds, making perfect tone with the ancient pines and giant rocks.

Another long silken scroll gave a realistic panorama of past scenes in the gardens and grounds

TWO SCHOLARS

of the Viscount's family. The ancient garden was on a larger scale than the modern one. One of the Viscount's ancestors was shown reclining on a stone couch attended by a servant, while a friend sat by composing poems, and other friends sat smoking long-stemmed pipes.

It was skilful work, for silk is a tricky medium for painting, but the Far East is essentially romantic. The pictures were all of actual scenes in old Korea, but—if only there had been a Korean Hogarth to give the other side of Korean life !

Now we were led into a small inner room where refreshments were waiting us. Our host retired to the men's quarters as a 'friend' had called to see him. We wondered sadly if the 'friend' was the ubiquitous Japanese interrogator. The two sons and the daughter-in-law ate with us. We knelt on cushions by a long narrow table spread with a cotton cloth —a concession to Western ideas. We were given fruit juice with a jelly prepared from a cereal accompanied by pine kernels. The jelly was served in black lacquer bowls. There were little round cakes made from pine pollen ; others were of mashed dates. There was sesame in some of the variously flavoured dishes. The meal started with sweets and ended with savouries. The central dish was filled with the inevitable fiery *kimchi* pickle. There were small flat cakes of dried fish, and thin hard cakes of dried beef. Finally as a concession to Western ideas, in addition to bananas and other fruit, there was a dish of strawberries and cream.

During the meal a very young serving maid in old-style costume stood at one end of the table and waved an enormous brilliantly-coloured, long-handled fan to keep off the flies. At the other end of the table a tiny girl, daughter of the son who was in Europe, waved a small fan. This child was like some Chinese fairy. She was fair-skinned, had prominent black eyes and small, beautifully modelled features. Her smooth glossy black hair was worn in a plait that reached below her waist. Her flimsy, airy skirt, tied under her arms, was of a beautiful deep blue. Her narrow-chested bodice was of pink silk. Her tiny slim arms seemed too fragile for work, but with an earnest expression she kept waving the fan to and fro until the very end of the meal. There is something extraordinarily appealing in small girls of the Far East. Their gentleness, their unself-consciousness, their delicacy of line and colour, and their modesty are exquisite—almost flower-like. It seems tragic that so many of them are gathered early into the oppressive sex life that has been their heritage for thousands of years. Although a new day has dawned for those small sisters of Asia, custom is strong and unseen chains bind their slender patient limbs.

When we had finished our meal, the old Viscount returned and we gathered again in the larger apartment. The boys entertained us by putting on their father's old official robes. These were made of brocades and silks of wonderful golden browns and reds. One, a scholar's black silk gown, had a Chinese blue lining. There were strange breast-plates of Korean silk embroidery and long silk robes of purple with heavy tassels. The hats were old-style, little, square scholar's hats of horsehair, with odd peaks at each side. Finally we were shown a photograph album with portraits of the present family including the son in exile.

We were preparing to put on our outdoor shoes and take our leave when the old gentleman had another surprise for us. He led us to the house connecting the men's reception room with the women's quarters, where we mounted a steep ladder staircase. Here we entered his own special apartment. He placed antique Chinese chairs at the window for us. From thence we looked down on the garden, and also on the beautiful valley beyond. Daily at these windows this old man sits and meditates on the tragic lot that has befallen his country. Here he may read in his Chinese library, but I fear there is less reading than sorrowful thinking !

While we sat chatting with the two boys, enjoying a cup of tea, the mother arrived. She was a tall, slim, graceful woman with a sweet expressive face. She welcomed us warmly. Koreans are open-hearted and even demonstrative in their efforts to show goodwill. While we talked through the boys with our hostess, the old gentleman left by an outer stone staircase leading from this upper room. Soon we saw him in the garden gathering a huge bunch of roses and peonies, and when he returned he presented lovely flowers to each visitor.

At last we took our leave, our host and his daughter-in-law accompanying us to the outer gate and waving us good-bye until we were out of their sight.

So much for the externals of our visit. There was no exchange of thought. The feeling of the place was tragic and melancholy. The Viscount was obviously living under restraint. To such a man who had been used to a life of activity, the present regime means stagnation. Every word these people speak, every person they see, every book, every paper they read, even every penny they spend has to be accounted for to an alien, and often an ignorant, official. They may not entertain a guest without being interrogated. They may not choose a site in their country where they may build. They are shackled, blighted. It is not life ; it is stagnation.

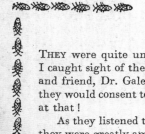 *See preceding colour plate*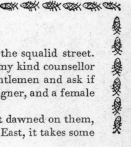

Two Scholars

THEY were quite unconscious of the interesting picture they made in the squalid street. I caught sight of them while passing on my way to a sitter and begged my kind counsellor and friend, Dr. Gale, to come with me next day to call on these old gentlemen and ask if they would consent to be sketched—and here was the problem—by a foreigner, and a female at that !

As they listened to the Doctor's explanation and the object of our visit dawned on them, they were greatly amused. The talk was rather long, for, as ever in the East, it takes some time to come to a point.

As I sketched, they did forget me and became lost in their classic tale. I hope when I get back to Korea such delightful figures will not all have gone.

Chapter Five   Independence Day

KOREAN SONG (Free translation)

Cruel hate its watch long keeping
Roused the Hermit from his sleeping ;
Human hearts were well-nigh breaking
But the twenty million waking—
Hope in their heart and One in Song—
Rejoicing, see them dance along.

Tok rip mansei !   Tok rip mansei !
Cho-sun, Chosun !   Mansei, mansei !

Our Freedom is a 'happy thought' !
With agony it must be bought.
Our bodies we most gladly give
If by our death our country live.
But, hark !   The Independence Song !
The signs increase.   How long !   How long !

Tok rip mansei !   Tok rip mansei !
Cho-sun, Chosun !   Mansei, mansei !

I AM listening to the story of how the Korean nation on that first day of March, 1919, like a group of happy children, shouted and danced and waved thousands of the forbidden emblem, their national flag, which they had been making in secret.

No foreigner was taken into their confidence.

The programme for the day had been carefully planned, and minute instructions had been given through the medium of their secret national newspaper.   Thirty-three leaders of the Independence movement had been chosen from a group of well-known and tried volunteers, some of whom had suffered at the time of the Conspiracy Trial.   Each of the Thirty-Three knew what they might expect from their Japanese judges : imprisonment certainly, and something that was harder to bear—torture.   They met at the Bright Moon Restaurant (Tai-Wha-Kwan) in Seoul, the fashionable and most imposing eating-house in the capital, where they had arranged to have a farewell luncheon.   To this function they invited several

c

Japanese heads of Government Departments in Seoul, all of whom declined. These officials sent, instead, a minor official to represent them all. Had these dignitaries attended, they would have been present when the Thirty-Three patriots read aloud and signed the National Declaration of Independence. The plan of the Thirty-Three leaders was that after luncheon and the reading and signing of the Declaration, they would give themselves up to the authorities. They knew that if they waited to be arrested they would be driven through the streets of Seoul at the point of the bayonet and prodded or beaten as they walked. With grim humour, therefore, they had a number of motor-cars waiting, and they drove in dignity to surrender themselves and their manifesto to their judges.

Throughout the morning there had been intense excitement in the city. Even the foreign

See colour plate opposite

The School—Old Style

Ha nal chun, da chi, tal uul, sarram in. In the bright hot sunlight this refrain came droning through the open gate of a thick white wall in a side street by an old city gate in Seoul. We peeped into the courtyard, and the picture tells what we saw.

The boys swung their small bodies backwards and forwards from the waist in rhythm with their chant. The old schoolmaster, wearing his indoor hat, sat motionless, like a carved figure. Perhaps he was dreaming some poetic fancy, for Confucian scholars are great verse writers. He had no need to worry, for the monitor, armed with a long bamboo rod, kept an ever-ready eye on the pupils. If a voice failed, or a small head turned wearily to one side or the other, the rod came down with a sharp whistle on the lazy one's back or whatever part was nearest. The small boy then quickly renewed his droning with some show of vigour.

After a time a second chant began and when the class made a mistake a cheery, rosy-faced, buxom young woman put her head out of an open window on the right of the courtyard and corrected the scholars. On the left of the courtyard open to view was the school-master's kitchen where his old wife was busy with the family meal. This interior looked dark and cool. The floor was of earth and the shelves of wood polished and dark through much use. The cooking vessels were of brass and the pottery a coarse red. Dried fruit, an ancient gourd, and a bunch of bright red peppers made colour in the shadow. What were the words the boys were chanting? They were the first four Chinese ideographs, and they mean Heaven, Earth, Moon (or Month) and Man. The boys who learn these interesting things have to get their knowledge by memory, and as there are thousands of Chinese characters, I fear the monitor will yet have much use for his rod of correction!

No girls attend these schools, but somehow the rosy-faced one had been able to pick up a bit of learning.

After the boys had got accustomed to the presence of the foreigners and of the artist sketching, and their throats had become dry with much chanting, they said something to their master. He shouted *Yobo! yobo!* and his old wife peeped in, reached for a gourd, and taking two covers from the mouth of a black jar sunk in the mud floor dipped the gourd into the water for each boy in turn to get a drink.

The day grew hot and heavy. Flies were constantly manœuvring in every part of the courtyard. No wonder if the small boys got weary. And all the while, through an opening in the courtyard wall, there could be seen an enchanting country with white-topped mountains and a blue, blue sky.

THE SCHOOL—OLD STYLE

community, who knew nothing of Korean plans, was aware of strange unrest and expectancy among the people. Crowds of Koreans in national mourning had been on the move from early morning. Finally, they gathered in Pagoda Park. Here the people were on the alert for the signal to be given when they would shout with one voice their national cry, *Mansei*, *mansei*, *mansei*; *tok rip mansei*! (Ten thousand years for Korea, Hurrah, hurrah for Korea.) While the swaying crowd eagerly listened for the signal, an alarum clock was set ringing and suddenly the voice of a young man was heard by loud speaker reading the Rules for the Day, followed by the words of the Korean Declaration of Independence. 'We hereby proclaim Korea an independent state and her people free! A new world is opening before our eyes. The age of force departs, and that of truth and righteousness comes in!'

The instructions to the people for Independence Day were: Let there be no violence. Let there be no riotous action. Buy no Japanese merchandise. When you shout *Mansei*, shout all together. Do not surrender to the Japanese, but do not resist when they seek to bind you. Do not strike back.

The following extract from the manifesto reads more like a poem than a political proclamation:

> We the sacred descendants of Tankoon
> Where all surrounding us is the enemy.
> Under humanity's flag let us perish.
> Shadowed from the great black cloud is the perfect round moon
> Which to us great hope will show.

There is perhaps no Korean quality that is more outstanding than the sense of personal dignity. I shall always remember one sunny day in Seoul seeing a procession of about a dozen or more Korean male prisoners dressed in wide pantaloons and loose coats of an astonishing golden-brown; on their heads cone-, or limpet-shaped, straw hats, straw shoes on their feet, and their arms linked loosely to each other by rope. The men were all six feet or over in height, and, walking in front and behind them, were four or more pompous little Japanese officials, armed, and wearing perfectly neat white uniforms with gold buttons, their heads topped by ugly, German-style, cheese-cutter caps, not one of them tall enough to reach the shoulders of their captives. The captives in that sad procession walked with an air of natural dignity, while their jaunty captors were overshadowed.

We take farewell of the Thirty-Three Independence heroes—and heroes they undoubtedly were—as they entered those waiting motor-cars, and with courage, delivered themselves into the hands of their rulers.

It was an astonishing and heroic uprising, showing a rare quality of imagination. The unarmed people were aware of the nature of the reprisals that awaited them. In the streets of Seoul alone there were some two hundred thousand people, and while the demonstration was going on there, the same manifesto and the same national song and shout of *mansei* were heard in every town, village and remote hamlet thoughout the Peninsula.

The Koreans had used passive resistance against their own Emperors. Crowds of people, dressed in national mourning, would come from the surrounding country and gather before the gates of the royal palace of Seoul. There they would kneel, night and day, bowed to the ground, in protest against an unpopular decree. The kneeling crowd would keep up their national mourning cry of: *Eigo, eigo, eigo*! for days and nights until the Imperial resistance was broken.

To return to the old and young demonstrators in Pagoda Park, who, when the voice of the loud speaker stopped, waved their forbidden flags which they had secreted in their clothing,

and leaping and dancing with joy, shouted : *Mansei, mansei, mansei ! tok rip mansei !*
After the first outburst, the crowd formed and re-formed in procession and set off in orderly
fashion through the main streets of Seoul : nobility, scholars, students in groups, youths and
girls wearing student dress, shop-keepers, artisans, every class, male and female, winding up
with coolies, beggars, and even the women of the town. It was a mighty and impressive
spectacle. Hugh Cynn, in his *Rebirth of Korea*, gives an eye-witness's account :

'Students with books in one hand and uplifted cap in the other ; stately white-robed old gentlemen
with their hoary beards flowing and their wrinkled hands waving ; young girls, their dark (mourning)
skirts streaming and upturned faces shining ; elderly ladies with their characteristic green veils on
top of immaculate dress ; mechanics with their rolled-up sleeves, and some of them with tools in their
hands ; sons of the rich, with shimmering silk coats flying ; rustic farmers with horny fingers and
bony arms, lifted towards the blue heaven ; stocky-limbed cart-pullers with their long white cloth
wound tightly round their head and hung loosely behind ; staid and substantial-looking merchants
and shop-keepers, some with their long pipes, and others with pen behind their ears ; plump youngsters
with their baggy wadded pantaloons ; some in wooden shoes, and some in silk slippers, smart-looking
young men dressed in European style, and men and women of every description, age and rank—one
and all, in happy delirium shouting : *Mansei, mansei, mansei ! Tok rip mansei !*'

The Principal of an American College for Korean girls told how her students had defied
her on the day of the uprising, and some of these girls escaped from college, in spite of her
vigilance, and joined the demonstrators in the crowded streets. The brightest girl student
was in prison. I was invited to go with the Principal to visit the girl there.

I had not then heard full details of the indignities, insults, beatings, and disgusting treatment that girl patriots had braved. We were allowed to speak to the prisoner through a small
sliding panel some inches square in the wooden partition wall of her tiny prison apartment.
We could just see the prisoner, who had to remain kneeling Japanese fashion, an uncomfortable
posture for Koreans. The peephole was so small that we could only see the prisoner by
moving our heads from side to side, and the prisoner having to stay in one position could not
recognise the visitors as only an eye would be visible at one time, but the prisoner knew her
teacher's voice and freely answered all questions. It was possible to make out that Ruth
had beautiful shiny black hair hanging in a thick plait down her back. She had a high-bred
face, round, with rich pink cheeks, glowing dark eyes, and very white teeth. Far from
looking unhappy, the expression of the girl's face seemed almost ecstatic. She told her teacher
quite simply why she had broken the rules of the college and how she had been arrested.
She also said that her sole comfort in prison was found in the twenty-third Psalm. There
was no bid for sympathy but rather an impression of triumph. The teacher wept as she
listened, but Ruth remained calm and serene.

Here is the headmistress's story :

'There were three days' mourning in all the schools for the Korean Emperor. The fourth
day was quiet also, but a junior teacher came to me and said : "The girls are getting ready
their northern head cloths (peasant style of head covering). They are wearing straw shoes
(sign of mourning) and they are dressed in white (national style). We must guard the gates."
At breakfast the staff warned me : "There's something going on. We don't know what.
The students from Tokyo are beginning to come over and our people will certainly be
influenced by them."

'We foreigners had no idea that there was a deep-laid national plan, nor that the girls

CONTRASTS

had been helping at night to print and distribute the *Independence News*. We did not then even know of its existence.

'The first indication I had of the strength and measure of the movement was about noon on March 1. One of the girls came to me and said : "Please, we must all go down to Pagoda Park. We are called !" I said : "You cannot go to Pagoda Park." They replied : "All the students are meeting there. We *must* go !" I protested, and finally said : "You will go only over my dead body !"

'Shortly afterwards some teachers called me to see a copy of the Korean Manifesto spread out in one of the girls' rooms. "Look at these words," the girls said in their simple way, pointing to the manifesto. "They are such *good* words. And see the names of our own friends and pastors on it. It cannot be wrong for us to go !" But I still said "No !" Then one of the girls said, "Will you not come too, and take one of us with you ?" I agreed, and chose Ruth. The girls, on the other hand, promised to do nothing wrong while I was gone and went to chapel to pray for their country while Ruth and I took the street-car for Chungdo.

'Before we had changed our car, a rushing crowd of students came down the street waving their hats and shouting *mansei*. There was a group of Government School girls in the middle and Ruth got so excited that I could hardly keep my arm round her. "What shall we do ?" she asked. "Go to South Gate," I answered. But there we met another huge crowd rushing from the police. She pleaded with me again, but I refused to let her join this rabble. Then we made for Severance Hospital, but there was another crowd there and many bayonets gleaming. At the next stop we got down, and I rushed Ruth along until we neared our own college again. Strange sounds were coming from the entrance and, as I reached the gate, I found the whole school standing on the terrace and about 200 schoolboys grouped in the grounds below yelling and waving their hats, the girls responding. I said to the boys quietly : "You must not come where my girls are !" and I kept pushing them back with my hands. "Outside the gate, please !" I said. "If you must yell it must not be inside the school grounds. Outside the gate, please !"

'The teachers, who had stood by not knowing what to do, now came to help me to get the boys out and we closed the gates. I set a teacher at each gate to keep the girls from getting out or the boys from coming in. I myself went to the upper terrace overlooking the main entrance. One of the teachers had turned aside for a moment and some girls who had been on the watch immediately escaped and ran down the street. A few got out, but I was in time to stop the others and then I stood with my back to the gate facing the rather pathetic group of rebels. One brave little girl stood defying me. Her father and mother had both been murdered in the country while her only brother had been slashed and beaten. Tears were running down her face. The other girls all kept shouting in chorus : "Let us out ! Let us out ! *please !*" The little girl in tears did finally get out and when I next saw her she was wearing prison dress.

'Meanwhile, as I was trying to assert my authority and prevent these children from escaping, we noted a policeman looking through at us from the other side of the gate. He waited a little and then went and fetched another policeman. The head man who had been watching us was a Japanese. The other three officers were Koreans. I am glad to bear witness that this Japanese policeman was kind and gentle. He spoke in a fatherly tone to the girls, saying that it was not a good thing for young girls to take part in the crowds and advising them to obey their teachers. When he said "How many of you will promise to obey your teacher ?" not one hand went up.

'The policeman then took his sword and began picking out twenty of the bigger girls, but I could not bear this and I appealed to these children once more: "Girls! You *must* promise to obey me. You know that I have never asked you to do anything wrong." At this they all threw up their hands and the policeman stopped segregating them. I appealed again: "Girls, you *must* know how I love you!" Once more they threw up their hands. The policeman then asked if they had any hidden papers. As I watched that man I felt sure that he had a kind heart and I said: "Some of our girls have gotten out of the gate. If you will give me your card I shall go myself to the police station and get the other girls to promise to obey me, and so get them released." I went to the police station on three successive days. Finally I found that there was no more hope, for by that time they had all been sent to prison.'

See preceding colour plate

Contrasts

SKETCHING in the open is often embarrassing. One day, seeking privacy to sketch, I entered an old-style, rutted, narrow lane where adobe walls surrounded straw-thatched dwelling-houses that might seem to be huts to the uninitiated. Although an unsavoury open sewer ran down the lane and a garbage box spewed its contents, peeps of courtyards revealed tidy and picturesque interiors well stacked with the usual beautiful great *kimchi* pickle jars.

Suddenly a woman appeared who glittered in the sunlight. Her gauzy bodice was of eggshell blue-green, and her cream gauze skirt, tied below the waistline to raise it from the mud, showed pale blue and pink silken shoes. Her black hair, like a sheath of satin, was wound in a coil at the nape of her neck and tied with a red ribbon, while another bow of red ribbon fixed the bodice of her gown. She had an obviously sick girl on her back, too sick even to glance at the strange foreigner. It would be hard to say which of us was the more surprised, but I smiled and at once there was a friendly feeling. Then a servant appeared and I became the object of their talk. Now almost magically a crowd gathered and its persistent curiosity soon drove me off, but not before I had got a sketch of the shining lady, though I had to forgo any sketch of the attractive courtyard. Note on the left of the picture is the hole in the wall, the only outlet for the smoke.

Chapter Six The Two Viscounts

RARELY can there have been a greater surprise for tyrants than this uprising of the meek-seeming, docile and despised Korean. That he should dare to shout *mansei* and declare his freedom ! Had the Japanese been wise rulers they would have 'let the people sing', but tyrants are rarely wise. So it came about that telephones got busy, orders were barked out from military and police headquarters, and men with swords, staves and, later in the day, others with long firemen's hooked poles, rushed among the unarmed, happy crowd. The police did not wait to make inquiries, but belaboured some, arrested others, and were specially brutal to students, both boys and girls. Girl students were dragged off by their long thick plaits of hair, but still they shouted *mansei* ! One little girl of twelve kept on shouting *mansei* with every blow she received and, when questioned by the policeman, she replied : 'I am so full of *mansei* that I cannot help it coming out !' Old and young men by the hundred were arrested. Soon the prisons were so packed that in some cells for a time there was standing room only. If the arrests were brutal, even worse treatment was given at the questionings that followed when every prisoner was offered the excuse—and refused it—that 'foreigners' and particularly 'Christian missionaries' had planned the Uprising and were at the back of it. Not a foreigner had been taken into Korean confidence.

Perhaps one of the most interesting features of the uprising was the part taken by the old aristocracy. The Japanese had given some of them new titles such as marquis, viscount, baron, etc. Some of these dignitaries now returned their 'honours' to the Japanese Government and took their place at the head of the national demonstration. Among this group were two old scholars, Viscounts Kim Yun-Sik and Yi Yong-Chik. They not only renounced their honours but sent a petition to Governor-General Hasegawa, giving their reasons for so doing. To make sure that the petition would reach the Governor-General himself, the document was placed in the heart of a spongecake which was carried as a gift by the hand of the grandson of one of the Viscounts. The following is a translation :

'A way of doing things is good only as it accords with the times ; and a Government succeeds only when it makes its people happy. If the Way is not in keeping with the age it is not a perfect Way, and if the Government fails to make its people happy, it is not a good Government.

'To-day when the call for Independence is given in the street, voices without number answer in response. The whole nation vibrates with its echo, and even the women and children vie with each other with no fear of death in their hearts. What is the reason for such a state of things as this? Our view is that having borne with pain and stifled resentment to the point of bursting, and being unable to repress it further, at last they have found expression, and like the overflowing of the Whang-ho River, the waves have broken all bounds, and once having broken away, its power will brook no return. We call this an expression of the people, but is it not rather the mind of God himself?

'There are two ways of treating the conditions to-day, one a kind way and one a way of repression. The liberal way would be to speak kindly; soothe, comfort, so as to remove fears and misgivings. But in that way there would be no end to the demonstrations. The use of force, on the other hand, that would cut down, uproot, beat to pieces, extinguish, will but rouse it the more and never conquer its spirit. If you do not get at the cause, you will never settle the matter.

'The people, now roused to action, desire that restored to them that they once possessed, in order that the shame of their slavery be removed. They have nothing but bare hands, and a tongue with which to speak the resentment they feel. You can tell by this that no wicked motive underlies their thoughts.

'The good and superior man would pity and forgive such as this, and view it with tender sympathy. We hear, however, that the Government is arresting people right and left till they fill the prisons. There they whip, beat, and torture them until they die violent deaths beneath it. The Government also use weapons until the dead lie side by side, and we are unable to endure the dreadful stories we hear.

'Nevertheless, the whole state only rises the more, and the greater the force used to put it down, the greater the disturbances. How comes it that you look not to the cause, but think only to cut down the manifestation of it by force? Though you cut down and kill those who rise up everywhere, you may change the face of things, but the heart of it never. Every man has written in his soul the word *Independence*, and those who in the quiet of their rooms shout for it are beyond the possibility of numbering. Will you arrest and kill them all?

'A man's life is not something to be dealt with as the grass that grows. In ancient times Mancius said to King Sun of the Che kingdom, "If by taking possession of the state you can make the people of Yun happy, take possession; but if taking possession will render them miserable, forbear to do it."

'Though Mancius spoke, the King paid no attention, and as a result, came to a place where he

See colour plate opposite

The Widow

THIS lady with the sweet, sad face is a widow from northern Korea. When she sat to be sketched, she had just come out of prison where she had endured torture. She looked serene and unembittered, although there were signs on her body—I was told—of the treatment she had endured.

This widow mourned not only the loss of her husband. Her only son had been taken by the Japanese, and she did not know if she would ever see him again. He was a patriot during the Rising.

It was summer when I sketched the widow, and she was wearing the traditional creamy gauze full skirt over baggy trousers; her bodice was of crisp hemp.

The people of northern Korea stick to their traditional style of head-dress. It was hot weather but the widow wore the northern head-dress which must have been very warm, more especially as, like most Korean women, her shiny black hair was long and thick and coiled round the head.

THE WIDOW

finally said that he was greatly ashamed. This is, indeed, a mirror from history worthy to be looked into. Even the sage cannot run counter to the times in which he lives. We read the mind of God in the attitude of the people. If a people are not made happy, history tells us that there is no way by which their land can be held in possession.

'We your servants have come to these times of danger and difficulty. Old and shameless are we, for when our country was annexed we accepted the rank of nobility, held office, and lived in disgrace, till, seeing these innocent people of ours in the fire and water, are unable to endure the sight longer. Thus we too in privacy have shouted for independence just like the others.

'Fearing not presumption on our part, we speak forth our hearts, in the hope that your Excellency will be in accord herewith, and let his Imperial Majesty know so that the Cabinet may consider it and set right the cause, not by mere soft words, not by force, but in accord with the opportunity that Heaven above grants and the wishes of the people speak. Thus may Japan give independence to Korea and let her justice be known to the whole world, including those nations with whom she is in treaty relations. Undoubtedly, all will grant their approval, and like the eclipsed sun and moon Japan will once again resume the light and splendour of her way. Who will not look with praise and commendation on this act of yours?

'We your servants behind closed doors, ill and indisposed, and knowing not the mind of the world, offer our poor woodmen's counsel to the state. If you accede to it, countless numbers of people will be made happy ; but if you refuse we two alone will suffer. We have reached the bourne of life, and so we offer ourselves as a sacrifice for our people. Though we die for it, we have no complaints to make. In our sick chamber with our age upon us, we know not how to speak persuasively. We pray your Excellency kindly to give this your consideration. In a word, this is what our hearts would say.'

Both old men were immediately arrested. Viscount Kim, who was 85, was too old and ailing to remain in prison so his grandson was imprisoned in his place. The grandson, I believe, became a victim of the 'paddle' and later died from his terrible punishment.

Viscount Yi Yong-Chik, after being arrested, was put through an interrogation, of which the following is an abridged report :

Police Interrogator : Do you know where the Korean headquarters are ?

Viscount Yi : Certainly I do !

Interrogator : Do you know who is at the back of this movement ?

Viscount Yi : Certainly I do !

Interrogator : Well, then, where are the headquarters, and who is at the back of the movement ?

Viscount Yi : With such a splendid organisation as you have in your police system, do you not know these two important things, even now ?

Interrogator : Don't gossip but answer to the point !

Viscount Yi : Well, if you want to know, I may tell you. But of course it is very secret so I cannot tell you openly. Bring your ear close to me and I will tell you.

(*As the old man seemed sincere, and the official was anxious to hear what he had to tell, he restrained his dignity and eagerly bent forward to hold his ear close to the old man.*)

(*solemnly*) Korean headquarters are in heaven, and there are twenty million Koreans at the back of the movement !

Interrogator : (*annoyed*) Have *you* not instigated this movement ?

Viscount Yi : Nowadays these boys get so clever that they never come for advice to old men.

Interrogator : We heard that you intend to go to Tokyo. Is that true ?

Viscount Yi : Yes, that's quite true. If I went to Tokyo I expect the Japanese people there would be much better than your people here are, but I have no doubt that things will be put right before long.

Interrogator : If you were not an old fellow we might have you beaten !

Viscount Yi : I never heard of Japanese honouring an old man ! I was informed, indeed, that in some parts of Japan when their fathers are old they take them to the mountains and throw them over a mountain-side so that they are killed when they reach the valley below !

Another answer by this old Viscount to the police interrogator shows the unbridgable gulf between the mentalities of the Japanese and the Koreans. When the interrogator asked the Viscount, in the course of his questioning with reference to one of the Viscount's answers, 'What is real power,' the old man replied, 'Real power ? Real power is what we are showing you to-day—the spirit of a united nation. You say that you have battleships, but you cannot break the spirit that unites us Koreans when we are calling *Mansei* all together. That is real power !'

Chapter Seven   ❧   Two Wise Young Men

I AM leaving out at this point two chapters on Japanese outrages because you have read *ad nauseam* accounts of the same kind of thing committed in Europe by the Germans. I will get on to my notes of the visits made to me while in Korea by a young man who came openly almost daily, for a week or two, when his day's work was done, to tell me of Korean hopes and aims.

He knew as he neared the gate that the two soldiers there and any policeman who might be patrolling the wide road, had an eye on him. He used to walk down the broad roadway at a dignified pace, pass the sentries with a word of greeting, and mount the long steep pathway with quiet dignity. He never hesitated and he never betrayed the slightest anxiety or nervousness. This young man had a medical degree and spoke English well. It may be that he is no longer alive.

'The more I study the Japanese,' he said, 'and we Koreans are always studying to try to understand their minds, the more I despair of any change in them unless they go back all over again to the beginning. They have begun life on a material basis. The object of our movement is not only independence but to help Japan as well as Korea.

'I see no way out of it for Japan. Her success is her difficulty. The case of the Japanese is almost desperate on the spiritual side. A change for modern Japan must be pounded into their heads by some gigantic force.[1]

'For myself, I would like to see a better Japan than that at present revealed to us. A better Japan would benefit Korea too. Now we Koreans know that with the Japanese it is country first of all. Morality, conscience, humanity, frank statement, everything is sacrificed for their country.

'Even their sailors scarcely had contact with the outside world. Then, suddenly, a few of them go to Europe to learn, and they think : "What can we get for our country ?" That was good, but the defect lay in this, that they saw only material good, and when they began to build their modern Japan they built entirely on a material foundation.

'When you converse with a Japanese, for a time the conversation runs smoothly. Then a question of principle comes up and immediately the Japanese says something so grotesque that you look at him and say to yourself : "Here is an altogether strange man. His honour, sentiment, all that is real, is under Government control." As I said to a Japanese one day : "What is morality ? You cannot

[1] A prophetic suggestion of the atomic bomb.

hold it in the open palm of your hand. You cannot see it, or touch it. You cannot blow upon it. You cannot take it from anybody, nor can you sell it. Are you blind to everything but materialism ?" '

On another occasion the same young man said :

'The Japanese in Korea lack political sense. They have no knowledge of the mind of our people. In this we are richer than our rulers. We Koreans see through Japanese pretence and realise that the material advantages brought to Korea are mostly to benefit Japan. Even the Japanese judges are surprised at the political understanding of our people. A judge who had been questioning a student girl was so struck by her answers that he turned to his officers and said : "Where in the world have these girls got their knowledge of Japan and her relations with the outer world ?"

See colour plate opposite

Temple Interior

THIS temple in Seoul is dedicated to the God of War. The carved figure with the black face under a yellow canopy honours the memory of a Chinese general whose spirit the Koreans believe delivered them from a fierce Japanese enemy three hundred years ago. Many people come to worship at his shrine. The temple is full of shadows and strange shapes. Women worshippers prone to the ground, their wide skirts light and filmy, look like flower petals fallen in the gloom of a thick forest.

Buddhist temples are often to be found on a hillside far from any town. The buildings are surrounded by a dazzling white-washed wall with thick, tiled coping. The rooms are open to the sunlight. Men dressed in white may be seen sitting on the ground at the entrance, smoking and talking.

In front of one temple there was a round lotus pond, and willow trees cast green shadows on the still water. It was April, and the occasional showers of rain added radiance to the scene. From the temple steps, cut in stone on the hillside, there was to be seen a far-reaching plain with low hills on the horizon. At another temple a giant figure of Buddha was carved on the hillside from the solid rock.

In this temple the visitor was free to look where he pleased. In one small room a priest, wearing the oddest ancient horsehair hat, sat telling his beads to the slow beating of a drum. The drummer was a pale young man with earnest eyes who kept his gaze fixed on the priest's hands. At each drum-tap the priest moved a bead.

Some women in single file toiled slowly up a stone stairway to a higher shrine. Their heads were black and glossy. Their skirts were stiff and gauzy as the skirts of a dancer. Their tiny feet were shod in delicately coloured silk shoes with pointed toes, but their ankles were swathed in great leggings of white cotton crinkled like the tops of men's hunting boots.

Before one shrine a tawdry trestle table was laid with a variety of brightly coloured cakes. Here two men were kneeling, one in deep distress, their hard little hats almost touching the offerings on the table. In another room many women were prone before an altar, while two stony-faced priests, dressed in gorgeous silken robes, chanted a monotonous prayer and thumped two hard-sounding small drums.

At times ugly and garish modern decorations spoilt the effect, and the irritating beat of many drums in different rhythms was disturbing ; but nothing could undo the peace-giving sense of being in a place far from the busy world of effort and danger.

Here is a saying that was written on the wall of a priest's room in one Buddhist temple : The Temple of Incense : from here you see the birth of the breeze !'

TEMPLE INTERIOR

'In their narrow minds,' my friend went on, 'the Japanese always say the same thing, "The Koreans must be assimilated or they must cease to exist." But they have failed to read history. They are really so foolish as to think that they can assimilate twenty millions of unwilling people. It is for this that they have established their spy system. To live in such an environment paralyses effort. You meet a policeman and he looks at you, follows you. You cannot walk from one house to another without being watched and questioned.

'There is one broad-minded man in Japan at the Imperial University. I look eagerly for his writings. We Koreans looked with longing towards such men when we began our movement for independence. Several of their writers expressed revolutionary ideas. "These men will understand and help us," we thought, but they could do nothing. Now we know that we must depend on our own efforts.

'It will be a great task for our Korean people to learn to build up good organisation, but they can learn to do this. With Japan it will be far harder to build up spiritual things.'

An interesting sidelight on Japanese character may be got from a talk I had with a foreigner in Tokyo. He said :

'May I remind those people who talk of Japanese Militarism that Japan has always been military. The hope for Korea lies in that other Japan whose people are as sick of militarism as are the Koreans. In Japan also brave men suffer from spies. One man for a rash word on Socialism has had a spy dogging him for ten years. He now finds the man useful in carrying his portmanteau and is no longer irritated by the spy's presence.

'Not only is there an enlightened Japan in the universities and in the schools. There is also a big body of Christian thought and feeling in Japan among both men and women. These people have expressed their indignation at Korean outrages. Again and again unrest rises in little waves like summer shocks that precede a big earthquake. Labour was never more vocal. Korea needs all her patience but the day of her deliverance is nearer than she knows.'

Coming back to my Korean friend, I remember his saying : 'History shows that any nation not founded on some spiritual basis always comes to grief. It may sound strange to you to hear a Korean pitying Japanese, but I assure you I am very sorry for them. I do not, of course, know all Japan, but the Japanese people here in Korea are a hopeless people.'

Having listened to the wise Korean youth let Yanagi, one of the finest young men in Japan, whom I knew well, have a hearing. He is a highly-cultivated Japanese in Tokyo and when still a young man had written a life of William Blake and had been a close student of Korean art. He protested in the press and elsewhere against the maladministration and cruelty of the Japanese Government in Korea.[1]

Physical courage would seem to be inherent in most Japanese but moral courage is rare. Yanagi San had moral courage. When he was a boy at the Peers' School in Tokyo, the national hero, Admiral Togo, paid a visit to the school and after he had addressed the assembled boys, whose deep reverence for such a man would amount almost to worship, there was a pause and young Yanagi asked if he might put a question to the Admiral. His question was :
Did the Admiral sometimes think of the men who had perished before Port Arthur ?
Some years later when on the death of the old Emperor the Admiral, who was a thoughtful,

[1] In my husband's *Foundations of Japan* (Murray, 1922 ;) there is a chapter on the life, personality and work of Yanagi. 'I am inclined to think,' wrote Yanagi in 1921, in a paper on Korean art, 'that we have paid, if anything, rather too much attention to European works while making little effort to pay attention to what lies much nearer to us.' He established a Korean Folk Art Society in Seoul.

sincere man, committed suicide at his home in Tokyo, it was believed that his death was in some sort an expiation for that slaughter. The unpretentious Japanese-style wooden little house in which the Admiral had lived in retirement became a national shrine and was visited by thousands who gazed with awe at the blood-stained mats which had remained uncleansed, a truly Japanese idea of reverence for the dead. The Admiral's faithful wife had committed *hara kiri* in her adjoining room at the same time.

I give extracts from an article by Yanagi which appeared in the Japanese press in the year of the Korean Uprising after a visit to Korea. Many other liberal-minded Japanese made protests.

'Those who have experience and knowledge of Korea are not deep or warm in their hearts. And for this I shed tears for our neighbour. Among the Japanese who live in Korea and speak Korean there may be some who have dug up old graves to study the old arts. This was done for science and not out of love for the Korean people. They were robbed of their historic treasures. Japan has spent large amounts of money and sent regiments of soldiers and politicians to Korea, but these have never been given with love in their hearts. Koreans in general are more hungry for human sympathy than for gold or politicians or soldiers.

'A certain Korean asked me the following question : "Is Japan educating Koreans for the sake of the Koreans or for the Japanese ?" Korean history is not taught, nor are they encouraged to learn foreign languages, but the Japanese language and the Japanese morality are forced upon them, and they are made to honour the Japanese Imperial family. It is Japan's duty to see that Korea's prominent place in the world of art is duly protected. The aim of education should be to enable their national ideals to live and not to destroy them. It is unreasonable for Japan to demand love from them by force while we withhold love from them. Christianity alone has given them love, and thus it is natural that the missionaries have gained their love ?

'If we desire to secure lasting peace with our neighbour there is no other way but to fill our hearts with love and warm up with sympathy. But at this unfortunate time Japan has thrust in the blade and made herself accursed. Will this produce clear understanding on both sides and ultimately make the two people join together with united force ? The Korean people think only of their manifold grievances which have produced bitterness and protest, and which lead to the demand for separation and independence. Naturally they cannot love Japan, and respect is out of the question.'

*   *   *

Although the Japanese officials persecuted the Korean Christians in their homeland, there were in Japan itself many sincere Japanese Christian people, a large number of whom attended church.

A great annual gathering of Christians of the Far East was held in Tokyo in 1919, after the cruel persecution of Christian patriots in Korea—indeed while it was still going on. It was not expected that any Korean Christians would get permission—even if they had the courage—to attend. One evening, however, when the hall was full, there entered with simple dignity an old Korean gentleman wearing his national costume, who had come entirely on his own account.

The 'tactful' chairman took occasion to say that as there were so many speakers present he doubted if there would be time for all to get a hearing, but promised to do his best. Many of the audience guessed that the chairman feared to let the Korean speak. He had no sooner sat down, however, than the sweet-faced old Korean stepped forward. A hush fell on the assembly. The whole congregation rose—a tribute paid to no other speaker.

YOUNG MAN IN RED

The old Korean shut his eyes, folded his hands, and in a clear voice said : 'Father, Thine be the praise and Thine the glory !' He then said : 'I grieve that none of my people are present with me to-day. I had hoped that Korea would have many delegates at this Conference, but my people are in great trouble. I ask your prayers for my suffering nation !' He then returned to his seat.

See preceding colour plate

Young Man in Red

THIS youth is wearing the official dress worn by his father and his grandfather when they attended the Royal palace.   The overdress of red gauze is worn above a blue robe, and there are small bags of white jade beads that clink when the wearer moves.   The belt is not supposed to fit the waist but stands out in a big circle.   It is made of tortoiseshell and leather.   Under the apron are two gold buttons which show the rank of the wearer.

The hat is of horsehair with gold paint.   Note the boots with their wide tops, which foreshorten the feet and make them appear small.

The official carried a white ivory tablet in his hand on which is written a petition for the King.   The surface can be washed each time a fresh petition is necessary.

Officials of lower rank wore a blue gown and black head-dress.   The rank is also shown on the breastplate by one or two storks.   Officials also had for their insignia, according to rank, one or two tigers.

When there were wings on the cap it meant that the messenger was bearing a message to the King.   He would leave the palace in a chair with the King's message ; he would not walk.   The King's own cap had wings pointing upwards, which meant that he got his messages from above !

On another day I sketched the Head of the Confucian Temple wearing a similar costume.

Chapter Eight   The Crusader

A YOUNG Englishman, Dr. Frank Schofield, the son of a gentle, retiring scholar, was at one time Professor of Pathology at the Toronto General Hospital, the largest and finest hospital in Canada. He gave up his work and the promise of a brilliant career, to join Dr. Avison in his medical mission work at Severance Hospital in Seoul, An American medical man of note said of Severance Hospital in Seoul : 'It is a model school more in touch with practical problems than any medical school I know. Their preventive work is excellent and they apply their laboratory work to the needs of the people.'

When only twenty-one, Schofield, full of scientific zeal, made some serum experiments on himself. As a result he was rendered lame for life in one leg from the hip joint. This physical handicap neither affected the doctor's cheerfulness nor interfered with his activities. Speeding along on his bicycle, he was a familiar figure on the Seoul streets, and was made lovingly welcome in many a remote village of the Peninsula. His love for his Korean students and friends, and his fearless determination to help them in the stress and strain of the modern world, did not keep him from taking a wide view of the political situation in Korea.

During the time of the 'troubles' of which we have been hearing, his unfailing advice to his young Korean friends was, 'Don't look to the West for help ; turn your eyes to Tokyo !' He believed in the power of that growing section of Japanese men and women who were out of sympathy with the militarists. To prove that his theory was right, he spent the whole of his scant holiday one year in the heat of a Tokyo August, tirelessly visiting Japanese professors, politicians, military leaders, and many private persons. Even at the time of the wanton burning of seventeen village churches in Korea by Japanese official orders, the doctor still had hope and was able to draw money, unasked, out of some Tokyo pockets for the purpose of rebuilding some of the destroyed buildings.

Dr. Schofield's open championship of the Korean cause roused much criticism and some enmity. Even his life was threatened, but Schofield was so obviously single-minded and had such a persuasive tongue and irresistible smile that, with his scientific grip of the facts of the situation, he found allies, even in Japanese officialdom. The doctor tackled Japanese officials of all ranks, from the Governor-General downwards. He made no secret of his having written many articles in the foreign press about the uprising, but the strategies he had to adopt before getting his MSS. through the Japanese Customs were never discovered by those vigilant officials, who passed one section of the MS. of a book baked in a loaf of bread !

One of the best things Schofield did was to get a friendly interview with the Military Governor of Korea. It was just after Japanese soldiers had set fire without excuse to the village of Chiamni. The three men present at the interview were the Governor, the Doctor and—to give him his correct description, the Official Spy. This is how things went.

The Doctor : (*lavishing his famous smile on the General, and turning to the Spy*) You have told the General who I am, have you not, Mr. O. ?

The Spy : Yes !

Doctor : Will you say to him, please, that I am a very bad man I have been cautioned by Japanese that unless I am more careful I may be sent out of the country, or bodily harm may come to me.

General : (*who doubtless knew English, after listening to the Spy who addressed him in Japanese*): Whatever have you done that you have such a bad reputation as this ?

Doctor : I have written many articles for newspapers, such as, 'Dangerous Thoughts on the Japanese Problem in Korea,' 'Paying the Price—the Lack in this Government of the True Nature for Successful Governing.' I have been in the country and have seen all the villages that your soldiers burnt. I have been to the village of Chiamni where people were massacred. I have taken photographs of the homeless people, and have written reports which I have sent to many of my friends.

The Spy : The General says that your reputation is splendid, and your character perfect. On the contrary, the General says that he himself is a bad man. He has a very bad reputation. He has done many wicked things, and has been threatened that if he does not stop and change his ways, something will happen to him.

Doctor : (*Bowing to the General*) I am very, very sorry, General, because in your case I believe it is true. I am very, very sorry for you !

The Spy : The General says, 'Please tell the Doctor that it is difficult for a General to be a good man !'

Doctor : I agree ! I had an uncle a General. He was Governor in Burma for many years. My uncle's life was sometimes threatened. But will you kindly tell the General that the first point I wish to take up with him is the persecution of the Christians.

The Spy : The General wishes me to tell you that there is no persecution of Christians as Christians. Christians have been ringleaders in this movement, and of course we had to arrest and punish them as other agitators were arrested and punished.

Doctor : Please tell the General that the Christians are a highly moral people. They are therefore interested in moral issues. The Korean people want to get justice and liberty ; therefore the Christians who know about justice and liberty are interested in the movement. These Koreans demand their rights as human beings. Christians have always caused trouble to wicked governments. It is Christians in the world who have liberated slaves. President Wilson is fighting Prussian militarism at the Peace Conference because he is a Christian and for no other reason.

The Spy : You have not mentioned Lincoln. I have been listening for that name ! Would you like to tell the General another story ?

Doctor : Yes ! Will you tell the General that I went to the country some weeks ago to preach, but the people warned me that if I preached there the Christians in the village would be persecuted. I then went to the gendarmerie to get their permission and the Chief Gendarme told me I could preach what I liked. I said, 'You must come with me to listen and if you do not like what I preach you must blame me. You must not punish the Koreans. They are my best friends.' The Chief Gendarme then said : 'Ugh ! The Koreans are all bad. They all tell lies, and they yell *mansei* !' The gendarme came to listen but when I left he tormented the women and children for two hours, and the people got so weary that they made up their minds I must not preach there again.

The Spy : The General asks what is the name of the village !

Doctor : (*to General*) General, I should love to tell you, but I am afraid if I do so you will send someone to 'investigate' and those poor village people will be beaten.

D

The Spy : Why do you say that ?

Doctor : Because a friend of mine held a prayer meeting in a Korean house and the pastor's wife and another old woman went to listen. Three spies entered while he was praying and brought out the two women. Before leaving the village my friend found the pastor's wife lying on the floor of her house. 'Mother, are you resting ?' he asked. She said, 'No, sir ! The gendarme came and beat me.' Your officials, policemen, gendarmes, one and all, hate the Korean people. You cannot rule justly if you hate the people.

The Spy : We are really the severe father to the Koreans, who are our wayward sons. Your missionaries are for their souls, but we are their material helpers. We are wishing now to love the Koreans, and we thank you for pointing this out to us.

Doctor : Would the General kindly tell me about the burning of Chiamni. I have the Korean story but I should very much like to have his account.

 *See colour plate opposite*

Korean Domestic Interior

A TYPICAL interior of the house of a well-to-do family. It was summer when I made the sketch and the head of the family was dining in the outer room instead of in the men's special apartment within. I had no interpreter so could not have any talk. Fortunately the head of the house was not embarrassed by my sketching him. A woman, presumably his wife, waited on him, bringing in the different courses. Men and women never eat together. The woman is to be seen in the kitchen to the left through the open door. Besides serving the meal she was also attending to a huge copper in the kitchen, just out of sight, in which the family soup was cooking. The fire that heats this copper also serves to warm the floors of the rooms, for under them the smoke passes to the other side of the house. In summer-time this may be trying for the passer-by.

On the white entrance wall of a Korean house are pasted coloured scrolls of cheap paper with traditional designs. When new the colouring is gaudy, but with time it fades to a charming mellow tone. One scroll may show a brilliant fowl, the symbol of time. A dog means that thieves are being watched, while the likeness of a fierce tiger or lion scares off evil spirits.

Roofs are of thick thatch or of heavy tiles, because of wind storms. A rich Korean is careful to build his house with a lucky aspect. Seoul is surrounded by mountain ranges, one of which is supposed to look like a crouching dragon, another like a tiger. It is lucky to build with the 'tiger' to the right and the 'dragon' to the left.

The men's room is near the entrance. The women's quarters are out of sight. A poor man's house may open to the street, but most houses have a courtyard and the homes of the rich have two, one facing the women's quarters. Here the children of the household play. Children make their own playthings. Girls play until they are eleven or twelve, when they enter the women's quarters and are taught sewing, embroidery, cooking and other household tasks. In better-class families girls are trained only for the home. They have to learn the tiresome etiquette of bowing and other traditional customs. It is important for a woman to sit gracefully. It is only when a father gives his daughter modern education that she is taught hygiene and the care of children.

No Korean wears shoes indoors and the floor surface is covered with a beautiful yellow waxed paper which is kept in a high state of polish.

The writing on the wooden beam of one living-room said, 'It is a pleasant thing to see green smoke !' which means smoke from the cooking fire.

KOREAN DOMESTIC INTERIOR

The Spy : The General says he will be only too glad.

General : For three days a reign of anarchy existed and there was a massacre of the Japanese.

Doctor : Excuse me, did you say a massacre of *Japanese* ?

The Spy : Yes, Japanese !

Doctor : How many were massacred, Mr. O. ?

The Spy : Two gendarmes.

Doctor : Were the Koreans very heavily armed ?

The Spy : They were armed with sticks and stones and various agricultural implements. The local police asked for reinforcements to be sent to Suwon. Conditions then quieted down. The Korean men were ordered to come to church to hear the lecture. The village men seemed very sorry for their violence. They then became almost anarchistic and fired the Japanese schools. For three days the Korean massacre of the Japanese continued. At night we arrested 1,600 in 61 villages. We released 1,200. The village people made a very strong fire.

Doctor : Did they attack the officers ?

The Spy : It was all confusion. Brushwood was piled behind the church and the scandalous element set fire to another village, which made it easy for the people to escape. This is a common custom in Chosen.

Doctor : Are the villagers in the habit of setting fire to *their own houses* ?

The Spy : While the lieutenant was talking he was attacked by a Korean. A row ensued and we do not know just what happened.

Doctor : What was the cause of the fire ?

The Spy : The superintendent is investigating, but we do not know yet, but we think it was due to a spark which came from a Korean house and fell on that brushwood.

Doctor : I see ! Did the men rush out of the church when the fire came ?

The Spy : No !

Doctor : Why did they not run out of the church ?

The Spy : Because they were all dead.

Doctor : They were dead ! How did they die ?

The Spy : They had been shot !

Doctor : Then the soldiers did not help them to escape from the burning church !

The Spy : The official report says that after the burning of the church the lieutenant divided the soldiers into two parties, one lot to help the people and the other to arrest the agitators.

Doctor : Why were two women killed ; one of them decapitated and the other shot ?

The Spy : Korean women become very stubborn when they are cross.

Doctor : (*with a winning smile*) *All* women are like that, Mr. O !

The Spy : They refused to obey the soldiers' orders and we are not sure that they did not attack the soldiers.

Doctor : (*to General*) Are not your Japanese troops very brave men, General ? How comes it that the village was burnt down as well as the church ?

The Spy : There was a very strong wind and it burnt down all the houses in the village.

Doctor : What about the other villages ! Seventeen villages in all were burnt down. Was there a very strong wind blowing through all of them ?

The Spy : It is an old Korean custom that when the police come to catch the scandalous element, they quickly set fire to their houses. This causes all the people inside to run out. The bad element then mixes with the other people and make good their escape.

Doctor : Was this custom known before the agitation ? Has it occurred in some other part of Korea ?

The Spy : The General does not know what we can say. It is difficult. He cannot quite explain, but we know that the soldiers went to 61 villages, and if they had burnt the villages 61 would have been burnt, whereas only 17 were burnt ! Therefore, the soldiers cannot have burnt the villages. The General does not think you understand how difficult it is to rule the Koreans, because they are such stupendous liars.

Doctor : Excuse me ! Did you say it was the *Koreans* who were liars ? What about the village that was burnt down in daytime ? Was it also fired by the agitators ?

The Spy : We have investigated but we have not yet decided what we can say.

Doctor : Will you tell the General that I have a story about liars which is much better than his story. Does he know Mr. X. of the *Seoul Press* ?[1] He is my friend, but he writes lies. (1) He says in his paper that this movement in Korea is not a national movement, and (2) he says that the Korean shops were kept closed because the shopkeepers were afraid of the agitators.

The Spy : The General says that he does not think that it is a national movement. A few agitators started the trouble and it spread from person to person just like the influenza, so we had to take drastic measures to stop it. The General says the shops were closed because the shopkeepers were afraid of the agitators.

Doctor : Please tell the General that he has been wrongly informed. The shopkeepers closed their shops to show that they were disappointed with his method of governing Chosen. Ask the General, please, how was the lieutenant punished who set fire to the villages ?

The Spy : He was punished most severely, very, very severely.

Doctor : (*impatiently*) All the Japanese tell me that. All the newspapers say that, but no one will tell me *how* he was punished. Was he shot ?

The Spy : He was not punished by the civil law, but by the most severe military law.

Doctor : But why will nobody tell me what was done to him ? The General must know because he is the man who court-martialled him. I shall never be satisfied till I know.

The Spy : His pay was cut in half. His pension was reduced. His promotion was delayed.

Doctor : And now, Mr. O., will you put your signature to these notes ?

The Spy : I cannot do that. These are just rough notes.

Doctor : (*smiling sweetly*) But the notes are true, are they not, Mr. O. ?

The Spy : Yes, they are true but they are just rough notes. I cannot put my signature. You do not understand.

Doctor : (*meaningly*) Mr. O. Have you been lying to me ?

The Spy : No ! I have not been lying.

Doctor : Well, Mr. O., always put your signature to the truth when you get an opportunity. (*Very unwillingly the Spy puts his signature to the paper.*)

And now will you thank the General very, very sincerely for giving me so much of his valuable time. Tell him I am leaving for Tokyo to-morrow. I believe that in Japan I will find men who are merciful and I will tell them the truth about the Korean troubles. The General must have many influential friends. Will he add to his kindness and give me his card to present to men of influence in Tokyo ?

The Spy : The General gives you his card with pleasure !

Doctor : (*smiling on the General*) This is very good of you !

Dr. Schofield said on one occasion to me : 'My method is to go to the head officials. I never deal with underlings. If I tell my tale to the chief man or men and show up whatever is wrong at the time, some of those men are glad to hear what I have to say as they would not have a chance otherwise of knowing what is wrong. Many underlings do wrong on their own account.

'I got the head official at Suwon to send yen 50 to each villager whose house had been burnt, and to send a rice ration to each family. This was kept up for a time anyhow. The Government ought to have rebuilt the church and every single house that was burnt. They did not

---

[1] Japanese official newspaper in Korea.

A HAMHEUNG HOUSEWIFE

do this, but they said they punished the men who were responsible for the outrage. They also said that they punished the men as hard as they could without court-martialling them. They could not court-martial those who were guilty because they had not disobeyed—they had merely overstepped their orders !'

Here is more of Dr. Schofield's talk.

'I wanted very much to see a pastor who had been beaten up by the Japanese, and I was scooting downhill on my cycle, making great headway towards the village where he lived, when suddenly, by the side of the road, an arm was stuck out and a voice hallooed : "Stop !" in the lowest form of talk. Here was I, separated from my partner with whom I had set out, and with no one near with whom I could confer, but I came to, and I said to the policeman : "Look here ! You must use 'high' talk or 'middle' talk to me. Then I will use 'high' talk or 'middle' talk to you. I am not a coolie. I am a British subject." He said, "Where are you going ?" I replied, "I don't know where I am going." "What do you mean by you don't know where you are going ?" I replied, "Just what I say. I do not know where I am going. You see when I left my party I did not know the country I was coming through and I have no guide. I just know we are going to see some beaten men. I do not know who they are nor where they are, but I want to see a fellow who has been beaten nearly to death by the police for shouting, '*Mansei !*' You see I was never told his name before I left." "How can a man be going to see somebody if he does not know where he is nor what is his name ? What kind of business is this !"

'I said, "Well ! do you think I am a liar ? I have got to tell you the truth." But the two gendarmes did not like this. I said, "Let me explain to you. There is a man called Mr. Y. in Seoul. We had a dinner party the other night and we had a great argument. He insisted that the Koreans were shouting '*mansei !*' for anyone who would give them 30 sen or candies. He said they had no patriotism. I told him he was a liar and asked him what Korean would be fool enough to shout '*mansei !*' for 30 sen when it meant a bayonet through his abdomen or being put in jail ! So I made up my mind that I would take a country ride and would ask the people if they knew anyone who had shouted '*mansei !*' for candies."

' "That's a very strange story," they said. "Well, you can call up Seoul and ask Mr. Y. as we are going to meet again in a few days." Then I just cycled off.

'I had determined to visit the burnt villages before the police got there, and I set off another day by bicycle, but the police saw me start. Some were already on their way on foot, but one policeman went back and got his bicycle and after that I had no peace. That wretched policeman got alongside me. "Lovely morning !" I said genially. "Yes," he said, "where are you going ? Very glad to see you !" "I am going into the country," I said. "What part of the country ?" he asked. "I am going to Suwon !" "I am going to Suwon too !" "That is very nice," I said, "let us go together." I was determined that I would get to that village before this policeman and before the troops reached it. I could see that this policeman was equally determined that he would get ahead of me. He was a great heavy brute and on the up hills he could beat me easily every time, but on the downhills he funked it and I sailed ahead of him easily. On the level we were just about neck and neck.[1]

'I could see that the policeman was peeved. Oh, how he hated my following him. He bolted off uphill again and when we got to the last hill going into Suwon, in the middle of the hill he suddenly said to me : "What is the time ?" "A quarter to two," I replied. Without a word he was right up the hill. I pushed as hard as I could up that hill, but I had been to that

---

[1] As Dr. Schofield was lame from the hip it was courageous of him to speed downhill.

village before and I suddenly remembered that an old woman had shown me a little bridle path that ran into the centre of the village.   The policeman on the fine military road thought he had me beaten.   I saw him sailing beautifully along 200 yards ahead of me.   Then I chucked my cycle into the narrow bridle path and let her fly down to the village and got there in about thirty seconds.   As I passed the people I said : "The police are coming. Soldiers are coming, but foreigners are coming too !   Don't lose heart !   *They* won't touch you !" '

See preceding colour plate

A Hamheung Housewife

THE women of Hamheung in Northern Korea are taller and straighter than the women of Seoul.   They carry heavier weights on their heads and their style of dress is unique. The head-dress, like a big hood, is made from a cleverly arranged skirt.

I sketched this woman in bright sunshine, but the sun's glare did not embarrass her, nor did she mind the weight on her head of the red lacquered bowl piled with wet laundry. She was careful to put on two jade rings.

The bodice of the Hamheung woman is much shorter than a Seoul woman's bodice. The tasselled bunch at her waist is part of her purse.   The skirt and pantaloons are of stiff hemp, crisp from the ironing block, but they crush readily.   On special occasions she wears garments of silk gauze.   While laundering, these women change into old clothes or work in their pantaloons.

To complete the picture the woman should have a baby resting on her hip or slung behind in a cloth.   It is not usual to find a young woman on her way to wash the family linen without a baby or babies.   In this same town I have seen a countrywoman coming to market carrying a live piglet on her head.   Men may carry eight or more small tables on their heads.

Chapter Nine   ʑ   The Military Governor

I WAS taken to visit one of Korea's famous Confucian scholars. On the beautiful hillside near his dwelling there were buried thirteen generations of his ancestors. The old gentleman, after greeting the stranger, turned to the interpreter and asked, 'Is that great War in Europe over yet?' 'Do you not read the newspapers?' asked the interpreter. 'And wherefor should I read newspapers?' queried the sage. 'Have I not the writings of the ancients for my daily study and recreation?' and he waved his hand towards his precious library of Chinese and Korean classics.

Young Korea also speaks with distinction if the accent is somewhat changed. Hear how a boy of ten described a hated Japanese schoolmaster: 'He is short-necked with a very thin face. It is the face of a beast gradually changed into a man. He shakes his rod at us. His eye is the eye of a snake looking through grass. His expression is the expression of a fox unhappily pursued by hunters and taking refuge in the cleft of a rock. When he looks down at us with wide-open eyes, there is no love that can be found in his whole appearance; only pride and anger!'

An old and tried British friend of Korea has sent the following note about a recent Japanese decree in Korea:

'In 1939 the Government General of Korea, under General Minami, Governor General at that time, adopted a scheme for making Korean surnames conform to Japanese sounds. Korea, like Japan, uses Chinese ideographs, and they are always used for surnames and personal names.

'In general Korean surnames, in their written form, approach those of China. The ordinary word for "people," as in China, means literally "the hundred surnames." They differ considerably in selection from the set of Chinese ideographs used by the Japanese for *their* surnames and names, and still more in pronunciation, although there are some ideographs which are shared by both peoples—evidence of racial admixture round about the seventh century A.D., when numbers of Koreans emigrated to Japan. Ironically, General Minami's own surname is one of these.

'The methods used for bringing about the change were extraordinarily subtle, but, at the same time, we may credit the Japanese authorities with some knowledge gained from past mistakes in dealing with the Korean people in such matters, as for instance sartorial reform. It was announced that there was no legal obligation; nothing except *persuasion* was to be used to get the Koreans to alter their surnames—but the *persuasion* was of a very effective kind.

'The appeal was made to (1) Fear of ridicule, (2) Fear of ignorance, and (3) Fear of accusation of "dangerous thoughts." "If you do not change your surname into one with the appropriate Japanese sounds," said the officials, "your children who attend school will suffer from the gibes of other children at the strange, uncouth sound of your Korean surname in its Japanese pronunciation when the school roll is called. Surely you have no wish to be classed with your ignorant, unlettered countrymen, who do not understand the intricacies of this question and the suitability of a change." It was easy to see that anyone who did not change his surname would be regarded by the authorities as harbouring "dangerous thoughts." We cannot be surprised therefore that after this kind of "persuasion" had been in operation for some months, it was loudly proclaimed that some 80 per cent of the Korean people had re-registered their surnames.'

On one occasion the Prefect of a city summoned more than thirty prominent business men and official Koreans to his office. Only twenty-four attended. Seven men were holding positions in the Government. The meeting lasted from 1 to 4.30 p.m. The Prefect said that great disturbance had arisen in the Peninsula and it was necessary that all who desired to restore order and were opposed to such disturbance should unite in petitioning for quiet. Hence he asked all the men to sign a paper stating the following points :

1. That the (Korean) Independence Proclamation had been prepared by low-down Koreans and that it did not express the sentiments of the people as a whole.
2. That if Korea is not joined to Japan it cannot get along successfully.
3. That if the disturbance continue and the soldiers and police are further annoyed, the people must suffer and cannot endure it.
4. That the disturbance will affect business very unfavourably and that it is hoped that peace and order will soon be restored.

Every man refused to sign, whereupon the Prefect said : 'Since you refuse to sign, there can be no other reason than that you approve of the Independence Proclamation.' One man replied : 'What ground is there for such a statement ?' Another said, 'Perhaps we may have to die if we do not sign, but it cannot be helped.'

On the following day the Japanese officer of the Business Men's Association invited eight or nine Koreans for a special conference. Four only appeared. The same proposition was made, but after all kinds of arguments the Koreans refused to sign.

Before leaving Japan I had been given, as I have said, letters and cards of introduction to various heads of Government departments in Seoul, and to other prominent Japanese there, but had not found it necessary to present any of them. At the Mission my sister and I felt so free that we had put off making official calls and no one had questioned our movements. After a few weeks, however, a Japanese official who had an ugly reputation in the foreign community began to come to the Mission and have talks with the Doctor who spoke with him in Korean. All his many questions had been answered until there was nothing new to tell, but still he called.

One day I found this man sitting in the verandah with the Doctor who said that the Military Governor would be glad to see me, I found that he understood English pretty well. I said I should be pleased to pay a call on the General, to whom I had one or two Tokyo introductions, and should like to go with him right away.

It was a beautiful sunny day, so I put on a fresh white costume, and after a little thought, decided to take some of my sister's studies of Koreans and Korea with me, for no Japanese can resist a picture.

THE COUNTRY SCHOLAR

The spy and I went by *rikishas* to the Military Headquarters, and when we got there the spy forged ahead through corridor after corridor, past gaunt white-washed rooms most of them furnished with office furniture made in Japan from Western models. Finally, we entered a lofty apartment which had an ugly thick pile carpet on the floor and heavy Western-style furniture. Several gilt-framed pictures in Western style were skied, and altogether the room was as un-Japanese as it was ugly.

The General was a fairly tall, even graceful man quite unlike the usual Japanese. The spy asked me to excuse the General as he did not speak or understand English, or very, very little. The usual polite interrogation began. 'How long had I been in Japan?' 'Where was my husband?' (who had been with me in Japan and was then on a visit to America.) 'How were some of the Japanese friends in Tokyo whose cards of introduction I had been given?' All was very friendly, but I had my own ideas about interviewing and I quickly undid the portfolio and put some of my sister's sketches on the table. The change was magical. Both men forgot their rôles and turned over the sketches one by one while I told them various stories about the different subjects. Even the spy seemed to lose some of his ugliness.

As I watched these two men I could not help thinking of the sad things that were happening perhaps at that very moment in that building. This was the place where so much 'questioning' and torture were said to take place. Many questions were asked about my plans, and when I had freely answered all, I asked the General if he would be so good as to give the artist permission to make studies of the interior of a certain Chinese temple in Seoul. The General at once wrote the permission on a card, and unasked gave me a number of official cards endorsed that I might use them when travelling about Korea or on my return journey to Tokyo.

On looking narrowly at the General it was hard to believe that he could be as cruel as he was reputed to be. It was the system that was all wrong and also the whole official attitude towards the Korean people. The General escorted me to the outer door and was courteous and kind to the end of our short encounter. The cards the General had endorsed enabled me to take all my MSS. and photographs telling of Korean suffering right through to Tokyo without having them challenged by inquisitive Japanese officials!

My journey back to Tokyo from Seoul—my sister remained to do more sketching in Korea—was uneventful. The General's card was useful protection except at Nagasaki, where there was a long wait. There, a persistent spy of low class followed me even to the restaurant where I lunched, and kept up his grinning, repetitive queries. It made me wonder how it must feel to be a Korean traveller without a card endorsed by a high Japanese official!

One of the first persons I saw on my return was our friend the American Ambassador, a wise, kind and able man, the late Roland Morris of Philadelphia. His greeting was: 'Thank God you are back! Now we shall get the truth about what is happening in Korea. I had two fellows from Korea here last week but they told their tale so badly I did not know whether to believe them or not. What *is* happening up there?'

Next, I saw a Japanese of influence, a relative of a previous Governor-General of Korea. The story roused him. There were even tears in his eyes as he listened, but he shook his head sadly and said that nothing could be done. 'Our militarists are mad dogs!' was his response. 'It is how they treated our own people fifty years ago!' It was the same man who said on one occasion: 'Our people are brave but they have not yet got the moral courage!' He also on another occasion said: 'We have not yet produced the altruist in our country.'

Our acting British Ambassador in Tokyo at that time was a man well-informed about the

Far East who had lived for years in China.   There was present with him when I told my story, the military attaché, a young but already distinguished General.   They made a perfect audience.   Our talk lasted until very late ; Korea was gaining powerful friends.   Not long after that interview, Japan—it was the time of the Anglo-Japanese Alliance—found it politic to relieve her Governor-General of his post in Korea, and replace him by an Admiral who was known to be humane.

See preceding colour plate

The Country Scholar

THE Scholar is from Wonsan.   His classic costume goes back in style 800 years, and he is wearing an ancient style of cap.   The staff he holds goes with the old-style costume. It has a white jade knob which its owner carefully kept in view.   The cord at my sitter's waist was of carmine silk flowing over the robe, which was a delicate shade of pale blue with a black binding, making a delightful contrast.

Koreans have always reverenced scholarship.   Their earliest records show the literati to be the most admired men of the nation.   It has always been the aim, therefore, of Korean families to produce sons who could show their scholarship as masters of the classics and also as verse writers.   Many are the tales of poor and virtuous scholars coming to renown, and of disguised princes proving their greatness by some intellectual feat.   Not only did men study to acquire learning.   They were equally desirous of writing beautifully.   The Koreans are noted for their skill in writing.   Trials of skill in hand-writing and verse-making were always a favourite recreation of the leisured classes.

It is a wonderful experience to come face to face with an aged Korean scholar.   He has a look of breeding, self-discipline, and sweet gentleness, and his manner is gravely courteous.   He seems to be in touch with some region of peace remote from the world of to-day.

Chapter Ten ❧ A Generation of Koreans in Hawaii,

By Dr. Alice Appenzeller

I T was natural that Korean patriots who were able to escape from their homeland should make a centre for themselves under the American flag. This centre is to be found at Honolulu. Under the energetic leadership of Dr. Changsoon Kim there is a flourishing Korean-American Cultural Association to which many foreigners of distinction lend their names and show sympathy.

One of the best friends Korea possesses is Dr. Alice B. Appenzeller, a member of the Association, who lives in Honolulu. She is the daughter of two pioneer American missionaries in Korea, was born in Korea and was for nearly twenty years president of Ewha College, the only college for women in that country. Dr. Appenzeller holds degrees from Wellesley, Columbia and Boston Universities. The following note from her about present-day Koreans in America is therefore of value :

'For a generation the international motley of Hawaii has included the figure of a woman in short white jacket and long, full skirt—the costume of a Korean woman, still worn by elderly people. Koreans came to these islands soon after the United States took charge, seeking refuge from the Japanese who were crowding out the owners of ancient Korea and running things to suit themselves. Seven thousand Koreans responded from 1902–1905 to the call for workers on the plantations. Here they could make a good living, educate their children in a free land, and perhaps do something to win back their lost country. The United States had promised by solemn treaty in 1882 to use her good offices to prevent the encroachment of any foreign power on Korea's sovereignty, but that treaty had been ignored in 1905, when Japan had been allowed a protectorate over Korea, after her victory over Russia. Annexation followed within five years.

'The Koreans joined other immigrants in the hard labour in sugar and pineapple fields in Hawaii which has brought prosperity to the islands. Many of the old-timers, who did not learn much English, are still on the plantations, but most of them have drifted to Honolulu and other centres. Many have established flourishing businesses of their own and are engaged in work for the Army, such as tailoring and laundering ; others are successful in furniture stores, markets, music stores, rooming houses, shoe repairing, etc.

'Their children were born American citizens, free from the hated control which the Japanese consul still tried to exercise over Koreans in Hawaii before Pearl Harbour. These children listened to stories of old Korea, attended Korean language classes, and enjoyed the spicy Korean food, especially *kimchi*, the national pickle. But they were proud to be Americans, and their parents were glad to have them learn English and all the wonderfu things that this new land afforded.

'Many of the second generation have taken degrees and excel in the professions which they are practising—medicine, dentistry, nursing, education, music, divinity, social work, law, engineering in many branches, accounting and others. It is a hobby of mine to note any Korean who takes part in public events, and a satisfaction to find their number is proportionately large. Koreans have a good physique and are excellent at sports. Many Korean girls are pretty and acceptable in work where appearance counts. A Japanese woman told me that it was because they ate *kimchi* that the Korean girls were so fine-looking ! The Korean population in Hawaii has remained at about 7,000, but most of these are now Americans.

'Through the years, the Koreans abroad have realised that only they could tell the world what was going on in Korea, for the Koreans at home were gagged and bound by the Japanese Gestapo, which practised its cruellest arts in Korea long before Hitler's day. They were untrained workers, these people in Hawaii, but they could give to the cause, and others who could speak and write English could proclaim the truth. So nationalist groups were formed and loyally supported by these hard-working people.

'But Japan was popular and her elaborate propaganda, derogatory to Korean character and accomplishments, was generally accepted. While calling Koreans backward and insignificant, she knew that their country was of strategic importance, and that this people, now 24,000,000, were strong, intelligent and resourceful. Her very denial of both education and arms proves that the Japanese are afraid to trust these weapons to their Korean subjects, for fear they would turn against their masters. By strictest censorship and espionage they tried to hide the Korean scene. But murder will out, and those who knew the situation at first hand, missionaries and other residents, brought word, and the Koreans in America were eager to be heard.

'But who could make people listen ? Who cared about Korea, or thought that her woes mattered much ? The sense of injustice and frustration which the Korean has suffered through those years when so few would listen, have made him a volcano of suppressed emotion. He *knew* he was right, that his country's independence was a pivot on which the peace of the Far East rested ; that if Japan remained in control nothing but war could keep her from further aggression in Asia. Alas, if America had listened to these warnings, how many precious lives might have been spared ! The Koreans felt as if they were shouting at the deaf, and that even sign language failed.

'Probably the most colourful political figure among Koreans who have been in Hawaii is Dr. Syngman Rhee, who came in 1913 and spent a number of years here. He is still the standard bearer of the Dongji Hoi which he organised. Fresh from study for his doctorate at Princeton under Woodrow Wilson, he had also a record of patriotic endeavour in Korea from his boyhood days. He became the idol of many Koreans, and his voice carried conviction as it was raised in behalf of his people.

'After Korea declared her independence in 1919, protesting by empty, upraised hands and shouts of "Long Life to Korea" against Japanese rule, Dr. Rhee was named the first President of the Korean Provisional Government, and later made Chairman of the Korean Commission in Washington. He organised a church, known as the Korean Christian Church, in 1916 ; but as many of its members were drawn from other churches, such as the Methodist, which had been serving the Korean people for years, dissensions arose. The number not accepting Dr. Rhee's leadership is now greater than that of his followers and includes the United Korean Committee.

'Recently a call to unity of all Koreans has come from the Korean Provisional Government in Chungking, which is sponsored by Generalissimo Chiang himself. The United Korean Committee now embraces all former parties except one, the Dongji Hoi ; it is hoped that before this article goes to press this party also will join with the others in leading the Koreans back into their own land.

'Meanwhile all parties, though they have been wasted by divisions, have held in common the great cause of complete Korean Independence. No Korean, from the oldest grandmother to the most sophisticated modern, ever loses their passion for the homeland. For this they sacrifice, supporting Korean troops in China, helping through gifts (there was a presentation of a cheque for $26,000,000 to U.S. Government for the war effort), by purchasing war bonds and through their own toil in war industries, etc. Their children were everywhere with our boys in the battle fronts of the world. One church, First Korean Methodist, Honolulu, has a service flag of fifty-eight stars for their boys in the U.S. armed services.

'Koreans do their part ; that is what a plantation official told me recently of his workers. An army post exchange manager told me that Koreans were his best workers. The head of a school in Honolulu told me that the Korean girls there had done more with their opportunities than others. Uncle Sam has been good to these children of his, and they appreciate it. They have always been eager to help him, and their services were of increasing value as the war approached Japan itself. Many of them are good interpreters, both in Korean and Japanese, which those who lived in Korea since 1910 were forced to learn. The widow of one of the Korean U.S. army fliers, who fell in Jugoslavia, is now studying housing in the University of Hawaii. "I think it will be useful in Korea," she said, simply.

'Individualists, incurable idealists, stubborn patriots are these Korean friends of mine ; generous, full of humour, hospitable, loving the beauty of the old, but quickly adapting themselves to the new. They have made themselves an important part in the life of these islands, and will spread their *aloha* far in the day when Korea can be called again, *The Land of Morning Calm*.'

See colour plate opposite

Water Gate, Suwon

THIS beautiful gate in its perfect setting on the outskirts of Suwon is typical of Korean architecture.

It is also typical of Korea to find women and girls wherever there is running water pounding the family linen against the smooth boulders in the stream. Korean women are supreme laundresses and their methods transform the coarsest cotton to a material of delicate beauty.

I was disappointed when I first saw this water gate the foundations of which dates from the fourteenth century, as it had been recently restored, but I consoled myself with the thought that the newness would wear off, and that when it was again necessary to rebuild, it would be built exactly as it was in the fourteenth century.

As noted elsewhere, there are Japanese who are genuine appreciators of Korean architecture. The oldest existing Korean wooden buildings are in Horiuji, Japan. Japanese collectors of my prints showed great appreciation of architectural subjects. I remember one day a Japanese connoisseur saying of one of the architectural prints, 'Korean line of roof quite distinct and individual from Japanese or Chinese curve ; you have got it just right!'

WATER GATE, SUWON

NOTES ON WATER COLOURS IN MONOCHROME

Nobleman at a Confucian Ceremony

THE Confucian Spring and Autumn Ceremonies have ceased even in Peking since 1920.

I first saw this old gentleman officiating at the ceremony in the Confucian temple in Seoul. There is little decoration in a Confucian temple, but the many pillars of this temple were of a lovely vermilion and the courtyard was always immaculately clean. The weather was cold and my subject wore his furred head-dress under his Court ceremonial hat.

At the ceremonies visitors came by Government invitation, and, Japanese fashion, officials attended in frock coats and silk hats. I was assured that the Seoul ceremonies were closer to tradition than those held in the Confucian temple at Peking. It would be difficult to conceive any exercises, as they are called, more antique.

Most of the exercises took place on a stone platform in front of the temple, and this platform was reached by seven or eight stone steps in front and at each end. The men were in groups of about twenty. They changed their robes many times. Some of the garments were old and had mellowed to a lovely sealing-wax red. Others were green and many were blue.

The music moaned and wailed, when the drums were beaten, boomed. When I was present at a Court dance in Tokyo I found, as is well-known, that Japan had copied much of early Korean music for ceremonial dances.

Some of the strange musical instruments at the ceremony at Seoul were made of stone.

I made an effort to sketch the unusual scene, but I found it difficult to produce a clear picture. It was all so entrancing that it was not easy to decide which scene and which robes were the most arresting, so I gave up and just sat and stared.

The offerings of uncooked rice, millet, beans, peas and meats, laid out in the school adjoining, were distributed among the College students, the professors, and distinguished Scholars and their guests. There were also rolls of lovely white silk which were offered at the close of the ceremony and afterwards burnt on a huge fire.

Later, through the kindness of Dr. Gale, the old gentleman came and sat for me.

A Game of Chess (Two Sketches)

THESE studies were made for my colour woodcut 'Game of Chess.' The models are typical countrymen. It is common to see men playing chess, often in the street. Koreans have many games, but I have seen only one for women. They have the swing—which goes far higher than ours. The swingers stand on the seat. As a rule the swing is hung from high branches of a pine tree, or from tall poles.

I have seen women swinging at various festivals, but I believe swinging is mostly seen at spring festivals.

Tong See, the Buddhist Priestess

THIS is Tong See, the lovable old woman of Chapter 3.

The Eunuch

ONCE or twice in Seoul I had caught sight of a man with a hairless face, a high-pitched feminine voice, and clothes and hat which seemed out-of-date. This forlorn figure was the last survivor of a group of Court eunuchs. For a small sum he was persuaded to sit for me, wearing the dress he had last worn at the old Royal Court.

Later, in Peking, I came across a Chinese court functionary who had the same lost look.   He still wore a queue and out-of-date clothing.   He even talked regretfully of the good old days of the Empress Dowager.

It is history how hired Japanese assassins rushed the Royal Palace and murdered the brave Queen Min.   An old American lady doctor, who had been Queen Min's physician, and was honoured by an invitation to the Royal funeral, held at midnight, gave me a thrilling description of the torchlight procession, described how the group of Court eunuchs marched with the other functionaries.   I had to hasten with my sketch, for he became restless.   The only link I could think of with his past was to paint for his background the view of the hill behind the Palace grounds.

A Daughter of the House of Min

THIS young girl is in correct costume for a young lady of high rank.   Her father was a relative of the murdered Queen Min.   I placed her in front of the traditional screen, but could not resist sketching her pretty shoe, although it is incorrect to wear shoes indoors.

Her father was the first and last Korean envoy to be sent to France.   He was the first Korean noble-man I had met.   He was dressed all in white and wore a *turamagi* of creamy gauze material.   I could not but marvel at his beautifully shaped feet.   His white bootee fitted so perfectly.   Had I been a poet I would have written an ode to his feet !   Although his daughter had an air of breeding, she lacked something of her father's rare quality.   His English was not very good ; he preferred to speak French.   I do not remember the conversation, but could never forget his grace in the setting of faded grandeur, a perfect background for him.

I met the daughter later when she was married and had a baby daughter, but I could not detect about either of them anything which brought to memory the exquisite picture I remembered of her father.   This girl spoke English well and seemed intelligent, and I was glad that she and her husband seemed to be real companions.

Riverside, Pyeng Yang

THIS Pavilion stands on the banks of the Tadong and the illustration is a sketch for my colour wood block print, 'Riverside, Pyeng Yang.'

The well-known city of Pyeng Yang is built on the site of the ancient capital where Kija lies buried.   He ruled in Korea before the days of King David of Old Testament history.

Kija's well is here, and its water is believed to be heavier than the water of any other Korean spring. Pyeng Yang has no wells.   There is a superstition that as the town is shaped like a boat, to dig a well would be dangerous.

Although, according to Eckardt, the Pavilion is only about 150 years old, the setting is so perfect that it suggests the site had been chosen with care at an earlier period.   The beauty of Korean scenery is sometimes so rare that the traveller is strangely moved.   Its beauty seems linked with a sense of the great age of Korean civilisation.   Walking or riding in the Western Hills near Peking gives one the same feeling of timelessness.   This sensuous pleasure is different from the joy one has in the scenery of one's own country.   I think of the peaceful, clean feeling of the English or Scottish rural scene. On one occasion I picked a blade of grass on the Western Hills of China and began to chew the end, when my companion tore it from my lips, saying that it was a most dangerous thing to do, as one never knew what noxious microbe might infest even a blade of grass.

The beauty of Korea and China in the hill country is so alluring that one longs to return before some now unforeseen project may defile it or destroy the strange fascination of these ancient lands.   One attraction of Korean scenery is the wonderful atmosphere of blue over the distant hills, especially in the north.   In summer it is cerulean but it changes into deep indigo in stormy weather.

Colour Etching   *Courtesy of The Beaux Arts Gallery, London*

NOBLEMAN DRESSED FOR CONFUCIAN CEREMONY

A Sketch from a Colour Print

A GAME OF CHESS

A Sketch from a Colour Print

A GAME OF CHESS

TONG SEE, THE BUDDHIST PRIESTESS

THE EUNUCH

Colour Etching   *Courtesy of The Beaux Arts Gallery, London*

A DAUGHTER OF THE HOUSE OF MIN

Sketch for Colour Woodcut

RIVERSIDE, PYENG YANG

PRINCESS IN COURT DRESS

PIL TONG GEE

THE UMBRELLA HAT

COUNTRY SCHOLAR BEFORE A ROYAL TOMB

LAZY MAN SMOKING

THE SORCERESS DANCING

YOUNG MAN IN COURT DRESS

EAST GATE, PYENG YANG

GENTLE IN CEREMONIAL DRESS

Some of the remains of this ancient city were destroyed as recently as in the Sino-Japanese War in 1894. The Chinese used the foundation stones for breastworks. The poverty of the people is seen in the appearance of the trees, which in the outskirts of every town and village have had their lower branches lopped for firewood.

The Princess

IN Seoul my interest was several times aroused by catching a glimpse of a delicate-looking, refined lady in an antiquated carrying chair. She wore on her head a black band with a tiny gold bird in front, the Korean insignia of royalty. This was a Princess of the deposed Korean Royal House.

Some friends, knowing how eager I was to make a study of the Princess, arranged a meeting. She was married to a Korean professor of a Christian college. I gave my word that her name would not be published if she sat for me.

The residence of the Princess was in an old part of the city not far from the Royal Palace. A sentry stood at the large Korean style entrance gate ; no doubt to spy on the movements and guests of the residents. Indoors, the house was in traditional Korean style—white-papered walls and warmed floors covered by yellow waxed paper. Along one side of the Princess's tiny, low-ceiled room was a beautifully embroidered ten-fold screen with a design of birds and flowers. On the floor were the conventional silken mattress and elbow and head rests. A book-rest of black lacquer with mother-of-pearl inlay was the only other furniture in the room.

As the Princess was in mourning she wore white only. In her shimmering gown of some gauzy material, with her sleek shining black head with the little gold bird, she had an unconscious air of grace, dignity and charm.

When sitting for this sketch in old Court dress the Princess wore a stiff blue brocade skirt very long and also very full. Her bodice was of olive green brocade tied with a red ribbon. On her head she wore a small black, red-lined crown with jade ornaments, like a 'bridal' crown, and there were the usual gold pins in her hair. On her chest were handsome amber ornaments with long pink tassels attached, and on one finger two huge jade rings.

Somehow the gown seemed to have an early-Victorian flavour, strange to find in ancient Korea. The dress must have been designed in 1896. This period is described by Eckardt in his *History of Korean Art*, where he says : 'When in 1896, in a final flare of vanished power, Korea was raised to the rank of an empire, the imperial throne was restored and furnished with European luxury.'

Pil Tong Gee

PIL TONG GEE (with a soft 'g') has not got a kind nature like some of the portraits of people on other pages. He is obstinate and self-willed and he can be heard grumbling loudly when his mistress sets him to do a small bit of work. You may even wonder why she keeps him. It is a common thing to surprise old Pil sitting in a shady corner at any hour of a summer day smoking a long pipe and looking over the hills of the city with an expression of deep injury in his eyes. Every movement of his unwilling body seems to say that he condescends to do this bit of work, just this once, but that it is far beneath a gentleman of his parts. Yet with all his faults old Pil Tong Gee is honest, faithful and a trusty messenger. He was trained in a high-class family, but since he became a Christian he has worked for foreigners.

On Sunday mornings he is dressed in spotless white, and looks clean and fine. He performs many small duties at the little Christian chapel. It is only on weekdays that his rough top-knot is unbrushed. One Christmas his mistress, thinking to please him, presented old Pil with a hat, but

E

he would have none of it. Custom is strong. Unlike old Pil, a gentleman would never be seen with his top-knot uncovered. Behind Pil Tong Gee stands his jiggy. The jiggy man is a familiar figure in the countryside. Hulbert describes the jiggy as 'almost ideal in construction.' This wooden frame is strapped on a man's back so that the weight of the burden fixed to the frame may be evenly distributed. So nicely poised is it that 'a man can carry any load that his legs will enable him to support.' When the man takes off the load the jiggy can be easily set on the ground and securely propped on its forked stick. A jiggy man, with the help of his stick, can easily rise with a weight of 250 lbs. or more on his back ; some men carry up to 300 lbs. A jiggy man will trot at the rate of thirty miles a day, carrying a load of 100 lbs.

The jiggy is the gardener's barrow, and the furniture remover's van. All burdens seem to be adaptable to the jiggy from live pigs to the huge native brass-bound chests or the precious pottery jars.

The Umbrella Hat

K O R E A would seem to be the only country where people have had the bright idea of attaching an umbrella to a hat. This leaves the wearer free on a rainy day to sit and contemplate nature, or think of his next meal, or just to sit and think !

When the artist spied this old man sitting gravely by the wall of his house one bright day, she thought how good it would be to get a picture of him. Courtesy suggested giving him a *yen* and asking his permission to sketch him. Now all that was asked of him was to sit still as he had been doing the whole morning, not a hard task, for he mostly spent his days in this fashion. No sooner, however, did this idle old man find that his sitting still was to be of use to someone, than he began to fancy himself and moved his head restlessly this way and that. He fidgeted and grumbled loudly and kept asking the guide how much longer he would have to sit. Finally, he said that he was sure his picture would be of great value to the foreigner when she could pay him a *yen* for doing nothing. He even asked if the lady would make a hundred *yen* in America for selling his likeness there. The writer feels sorry to have to give such a sad account of this old man who looks such a fine fellow in the picture, but old men in Korea are made so much of that they sometimes get too high an opinion of their worth.

Country Scholar Before a Royal Tomb

H E R E is my Wonsan (of "Eastern Windows") Scholar in another rôle. I had told him that of all his numerous family I only wished to sketch him, and I had almost finished the first sketch when he suggested that we should pay a visit to his ancestral tombs. I should have preferred to finish the sketch that I had begun but as he was proving such a perfect collaborator I did not demur.

He took off the indoor headdress, which belonged to the same period as the 800-year-old-style robe, and donned the cap or hood as seen in the sketch. He also put on his outdoor shoes and we set off with his grandsons following.

The tombs were in a perfect setting. I agree with Hulbert who writes, 'It is a question whether the shape and appointments of a Korean grave are not the most beautiful in the world.'

The Scholar's grandsons took off their shoes and bowed low before the graves, which were shaped in exact hemispheres. In front of these were large oblong stones which held the small dishes used for the offerings of rice and wine which are made on special anniversaries.

As the Scholar made such a perfect picture on the hillside, I have placed him in this sketch standing before a Royal tomb. Royal tombs are always set amid fine scenery and generally on a hillside. Like those of Chinese royalty of old, Korean royal tombs have stone figures of horses and sheep, flanked by effigies of civil and military officials.

Lazy Man Smoking

I T is a restful sight at the open door of a Korean house to see within an old man smoking his long-stemmed pipe. It is correct style for a gentleman to have his servant light his pipe for him. But the stem is so long that it is hard to see how he could possibly light it himself !

As you may see in another picture, men may smoke these long-stemmed pipes even while doing such work as shoe-making. But the really happy smoker is he who sits doing nothing but taking long-drawn puffs from his prized pipe and gazing into dreamland.

The cheapest pipes are made of bamboo. Sometimes they have designs burnt into them. Some are carved. Others are plain but tipped with brass or silver. Some pipes are partly made of soap-stone inlaid with blue. Women's pipes are painted, or rather the old-style ones were. Ordinarily, the modern young woman student does not smoke.

Koreans grow their own tobacco, so they have it mild or strong to suit their taste.

The old gentleman of the picture may possibly be one of the large number of men who live on the eternal credit of the family system, where every responsibility is shared and the male burden is often light compared with the efforts of the women of the family. But a new age has begun and the young men are mostly showing themselves equal to their family burdens.

The Sorceress [See Chapter 3]

Young Man in Court Dress

T H I S youth is wearing the official dress that one of his ancestors wore at the old Court of Korea. He is a brother of the young man in red facing page 46, who is also wearing the Court dress of an ancestor.

The background is the ancient Gate in the huge square in front of the Royal Palace. The Japanese displaced this Gate by a disfiguring modern building, and put the ancient gateway in a lane running by the side of the Palace wall. This was a characteristic piece of injustice which expressed Japanese jealousy of Korean national treasures.

The robe the boy is wearing is of blue gauze, that of a minor Court official. There would be one or two storks or tigers embroidered on the breastplate according to rank.

When the young man posed for me, he acted as if memorising his speech before entering the Royal presence. There would be chair-bearers in attendance.

To-day only a bridegroom wears such a dress. I have often seen bridegrooms on horseback thus clothed. The robe is hired by the lower classes.

East Gate, Pyeng Yang

T H I S is a reproduction of my colour wood block print of the East Gate, Pyeng Yang, and it is the last remaining gate of the old wall, built in 1392. It lacks the majesty of the grand East Gate of Seoul, but though simple in style it has an impressive sense of great age. It would seem to carry out what Eckhart writes about Korean architecture : 'Although Korea received from China the essentials of her architectural style, it was in a much simpler, nobler, and more restrained form.'

I have shown it in winter, remote and lonely, but it was by no means so when I sketched it. The spot is popular, for it lies on the way to the river, and there is a constant procession of women going to and coming from the water, in which they belabour their house-linen on smooth stones.

The setting up of a sketching stool was a signal for a gaping crowd to appear from nowhere ! On this occasion my audience, mostly of boys and old men, grew to such proportions that my sister, who was with me, drew a line in the dust to show the onlookers how near they might come. When we said, 'Keep back, please !' or 'Out you go, young man !' the boys would yell with laughter and cleverly imitate our voices so we had to laugh with them.

In the end I had to stop and return another day at cock crow to avoid the crowd. But it seems impossible for travellers to keep their movements secret in the Far East, and an interested crowd always arrived.

Gentle in Ceremonial Dress

GENTLE is wearing the correct ceremonial dress for a young lady of the upper classes. Her great-grandmother was most careful to arrange her skirt, and it was she who placed the disfiguring white linen tie to fall exactly over the front of the skirt.

Gentle sat like a statue, unusual for a Korean woman, except on the wedding day. Unlike Japanese women who also sit on the floor—kneeling always with their feet slightly bent and the toes showing behind, and never changing their position—the Korean women sit cross-legged and change the position when their legs get tired. I have often surreptitiously sketched countrywomen sitting in church on the floor and noted with amusement the upheaval made by their bunchy skirts over equally bunchy pants during a change of position.

Although Korean girls have always been trained to take an inferior place to their brothers, they proved themselves heroic during the Independence Uprising, braving sadistic treatment from their gaolers, and taking an equal share with the men and youths in the national underground work, carried secret messages and helped with the printing and distribution of the patriots' newspaper. Whenever and wherever Korean women have had a chance to show their mettle they have risen to the test.

Like most Far Eastern people, Koreans have usually histrionic talent. One of the most delightful performances I ever saw was given by Korean schoolgirls. It was a dramatisation of Louisa Alcott's *Little Women* ! The oddly assorted clothing over unbraced youthful figures with overflowing curves was forgotten in the sincerity and exquisite sympathy for the characters the girls were portraying. The feeling was especially fine in the last scene where Beth lay dying.

Another performance, this time by twelve little girls from the Salvation Army, who sang in strange English a chorus ending, 'We want to be happy,' was a moving experience. Let us hope they are happy now that they are free from the bondage of the Japanese. These girls had been picked up in the gutter by the Army, their parents being too poor to keep them.

Shoes and Shoemakers

WHEN you visit Korea you may think that you have never before seen so many tall people with such slender feet. It is common to find a big man sitting next you in the street-car who has dainty feet that many a woman would like to own.

In place of stockings the Koreans wear a tight-fitting soft cotton bootee. This is seamed over the instep and is loose at the ankle. Strangers judge a woman by the neatness of the fit. There must not be the slightest wrinkle over the instep.

A lady's shoe is a beautiful, ornamental thing. It may be made of silk with leather sole. It is whitened with finely ground clam shell, the same powder as that used for powdering the face. A woman's pretty shoe of part silk, part leather, part paper is like a bit of mosaic. The workmanship seems perfect.

SHOES AND SHOEMAKERS

Colour Etching   *Courtesy of The Beaux Arts Gallery, London*

THE FLAUTIST

SCHOOLS OLD AND NEW

THE WARRIOR

THE GREEN CLOAK

SEE SAW

THE FARMER

THE MAT SHOP

No lady goes to the shop to buy her own shoes. Instead, her husband measures her size with a stick and shows this to the shoemaker. Shoes are the same shape for both feet. There are no rights and lefts.

Even the wooden shoes are beautifully made. All children have wooden shoes in wet weather. The three men in the picture are making wooden shoes. They work quickly and with sureness. The man at the back is cutting blocks of wood roughly the size of the shoe to be made. The old man is the most expert artisan and does all the fine finishing work. As the men work they smoke. Their long pipes are kept in place by resting them on little cradles of leather swung from the ceiling. Shoe-makers are of the lowest social class.

Upper class people do not buy wooden shoes. Leather shoes are much easier to wear. The leather for shoe-making is prepared in the winter and when it is ready it is as hard as wood and can never become unshapely. Leather shoes are generally coloured yellow with touches of red. Men's shoes have black felt outside and leather inside. Women's shoes are always lined with white, and when they are black outside they have white toes and edges. Shoes all have an upward curve at the toe that rather reminds one of Turkish footgear. Even the straw shoes or sandals worn by people in mourning and by country folk and poor people in towns are beautiful. Japanese introduced rubber shoes which were very popular. During the War years Koreans had to resort to wooden shoes again.

The Flautist

THIS musician was a member of the Korean Court School of Music. As there was no longer a Korean Court the Japanese Government sponsored the movements of the musicians.

I was fortunate in getting this man and several other members of the school to sit for me, but I was not able at the time to get a musician who could play some of the rare ancient instruments that I had seen and heard at a Confucian ceremony.

The most unusual instrument was made of triangular-shaped stones that looked like coarse jade ; as found in tombs ; the stones were hung on wooden frames and when skilfully struck gave out the full scale. The tone was lovely. Such sounds were mostly used as accents with the wailing flute. There were also coloured wooden clappers in the form of ducks. These were clapped together at each varying posture of the twenty or more gaily-robed men—right to left—forward and backward. There were drums with carved birds on their frames. Some of the drums gave out a hard wooden sound, but there were many different kinds of drums. The notes of the flute always rose above other sounds, and excelled in beauty.

This flautist was a fine artist and his courtly manners bespoke a man of breeding. Koreans, like Japanese, have graceful hands, and it was a pleasure to watch the play of the flautist's sensitive fingers.

Schools Old and New

ON my first visit to Seoul I had gone in search for subjects one lovely spring morning and had stumbled on this perfect setting for a group of Korean boys in their picturesque dress. The old Korean temple was evidently being used by the Japanese as a 'transition' school before they had had time to build fast enough another of their soul-destroying cement and concrete, regimented schools. Some of the boys were quite young, hence the lovely bright colours of their little jackets, and they all wore baggy white pants.

The military figure of the teacher, complete with sword, made a ludicrous picture against the peaceful background of the painted temple. He shouted his commands at the small boys as if they were on parade. How the bigger boys must have longed for the old style Confucian school with its easy discipline and homely surroundings !

When visiting Korea a few years later the clothing of schoolboys had all been changed. They were dressed in Japanese style, uniform complete with the hideous Japanese 'cheese-cutter' cap.

Now that Korea is free from Japan's grip, will they revert to old style national dress or will it be easier to carry on as the Japanese began ? Will they be able to rid themselves of Japanese ugliness, not only in dress but in architecture ? Who are to be their wise counsellors ?

The Warrior

T H I S man is wearing the uniform of a soldier of the last Korean reign. The dress was actually worn at Court about fifty years ago. The man who sat for the sketch was rather proud of the costume and was careful, as you see, to hold his stick in the correct way. He was proud of his sword also.

The hat seemed the most un-martial part of the costume. The blue, round pom-pom-looking ornament at the right side of the hat was of blue plush made from the feathers of some bird unknown to me ; but the tuft on the ornament, as you see, was of peacock's feathers.

Note the arrows peeping over his right shoulder and the antique amber beads at the man's neck fixed to the brim of his hat. See also his clumsy soft boots. The last thing he put on was the blue sash. When he had tied this round his waist he was ready for battle !

The following extract from Hulbert's *Passing of Korea* throws some light on the cause of Korean contempt for soldiering and pride in scholarship : 'During the first three centuries of Koryu's power (this means from 918 to 1392) there was a gradual evolution of the social system, based mainly upon Chinese ideals, modified by Buddhistic precepts. The national examination became a fixture, though it presented some unimportant contrasts to the Chinese system. It is this institution that must answer for the absence of any such martial spirit as that which Japan displayed.

The literary element became the leading element in the Government, and scholarship the only passport to official position. The soldier dropped to a place inferior to that of any other reputable citizen, and from that time to this the soldier in Korea, as in China, has been considered but one step above the beggar.'

The Green Cloak

T H E green cloak worn over the head is correct street costume. It is worn by women of the merchant class. Once it could only be worn by wives of a certain class of warrior. The green cloak holds in memory some brave deed of long ago, and the red cuffs and ribbons are symbolic of blood having been shed by some hero. The cloak is lined with white silk and has red ribbons to tie it. It is worn over the head and shoulders. The sleeves hang empty.

No woman may wear a green cloak until she is married. When the pretty wife of a merchant puts on this wrap, she covers her face all except her eyes and grasps the skirt of the cloak with her hand.

The green cloak was quite a common sight when I first visited Korea, but gradually the custom changed and on my last visit to Seoul in 1936 I had to wait for some weeks before being able to point one out to a newcomer who was with me.

See-Saw

T H E S E two girls are playing at a kind of jumping see-saw. The Korean name for the game is *Noltununga*, and it is played chiefly in springtime. This is the only girls' game in Korea, with the exception of swinging.

In old Korea, girls of good family were kept, after the age of ten or eleven, in the women's quarters, where they had only a closed courtyard to walk in. Sometimes the older girls would play this jumping game and jump high enough to peep over the courtyard wall. This was their chance of getting a glimpse of the outside world.

Girls were taught from their childhood that they were inferior to boys. Often girls were not even given names, but were called by numbers, as No. 1 girl, No. 2 girl, and so on, according to their order in the family. *Noltununga*, as you see, is a dangerous game and needs skill. The see-saw board springs lightly on a heap of rice matting. The girls jump in their hard wooden shoes. As one girl comes down with all her weight on the end of the wooden board the other girl shoots high up in the air, sometimes seeming to jump her own height. Then she has to come down neatly on her end of the board and send the other girl up. And so on they go with amazing speed. Sometimes the excitement of the game is too much for one of them and she comes slap down on the ground. In this way girls often break a limb, or hurt their spines, or knock out their teeth, but the fear of such accidents does not keep them from playing.

The girls' short jackets are the same shape as those worn by their mothers and grandmothers. Under wide skirts they wear long, very wide, balloon-like trousers. When the upper skirt is of thin transparent material the trousers are plainly seen and the effect is quaint.

The little girl who is holding the baby in this picture has a name, but it is not much better than having a number, for her name means Sorry ! She was given this name because she was the fifth girl in the family.

This house is high up on the hillside, and in the distance can be seen a lovely mountain range. The fence is made from broom corn.

The Farmer

T H I S young north countryman who used to bring his produce to the house where I stayed in Wonsan took his sitting seriously and, to my regret, arrived on the day appointed spotless in freshly laundered pants and waistcoat.

Nothing could be done about it, and here he is all strained attention, with hands in a typical Korean pose. Both the Scholar and the Princess held the same attitude. As the laws of deportment both in China and in Korea are rigid, I made a point of never posing my models, leaving this to one of the female heads of the house who would voluntarily titivate the model for me. The farmer here is dressed as he would look when going to town.

The background is of a landscape ready for rice planting. It looks serene, for the picture can give no hint of the odours, nor of the grievous labour. As usual, the pine-tree has been shorn of its lower branches for firewood.

The patient bullock is used in turn as a bulldozer or a tractor ; to harrow or to plough ; also as a means of transport. Korea's chief fuel is brushwood and it is common to see a bullock with a cargo of brushwood so big that only his four legs are visible.

Korean rice is said by connoisseurs to excel in flavour both Chinese and Japanese rice.

The Mat Shop

K O R E A N shops to-day are rather dull, for the Japanese took over all the business in the modern part of Seoul, with the exception of that in old style hats, grass mats and domestic brass. I sketched the prettiest mat shop I could find. It was painted a lovely green. In the front of the shop there are rolls of the fine rush matting with coloured designs used in every house to keep clean the yellow waxed paper that covers the stone floors. Sleeping mattresses are spread on these floors at night.

The bunches of grass hanging in the window are ready to be used for shoe-making and for mats. The flat baskets are used for holding grain and red peppers, beans and so on. The red wooden bowls carry the family linen to be washed in a nearby stream. The woman in the foreground, with her baby tied behind, is on her way to launder the family clothes.

The wooden shoes have just come from the shoe carver and have not yet been covered by the fine dust that is everywhere in streets and roadways. At the door is a blue-backed decorated screen, sometimes embroidered, that is to be seen in every home. It is always in the place of honour. The pretty brass trays are for cakes and other food and are always used at marriage feasts. Brass is in constant use. Even rice and soup are served in brass bowls. There is a national emblem on the pretty coloured fan. The shopkeeper and his customer, both in white, are having a leisurely talk over the purchase.

Made and Printed in Great Britain at St. Albans by *The Mayflower Press* (*of Plymouth*). William Brendon & Son, Ltd.